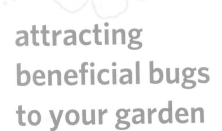

attracting
beneficial bugs
to your garden

attracting beneficial bugs to your garden

a natural approach to pest control

Jessica Walliser

Timber Press
Portland / London

Frontispiece Gardens aren't just for people. They are a refuge for a broad assortment of insects otherwise displaced by loss of their traditional habitat. Creating landscapes that support these creatures not only provides them with a safe haven but also can help restore ecological balance.

Published in 2014 by Timber Press, Inc.

Photography credits appear on page 239.
Illustrations by Colin Kinsley

The Haseltine Building
133 S.W. Second Avenue, Suite 450
Portland, Oregon 97204-3527
timberpress.com

6a Lonsdale Road
London NW6 6RD
timberpress.co.uk

Printed in China
Book design by Breanna Goodrow

Library of Congress Cataloging-in-Publication Data
Walliser, Jessica.
  Attracting beneficial bugs to your garden : a natural approach to pest control / Jessica Walliser. – 1st ed.
       p. cm.
  Includes index.
  ISBN 978-1-60469-388-1
  1. Garden pests–Biological control. 2. Beneficial insects. I. Title.
  SB603.5.W35 2014
  628.9'6–dc23
                         2013015303

contents

introduction

how a horticulturist came to bugs

don't be fooled by the title of this book. Yes, it is about bugs—about understanding their value to the garden and to the world. It is about encouraging the beneficial ones in hopes of mitigating the pesty ones. It is about learning to recognize how beneficial insects work, what some of them look like, and how they influence the delicate balance of the garden. But this book is also about plants. You cannot have one without the other, after all. The intent of these pages is to partner the two, to make your garden a place where bugs are welcome and a home for plants that provide for all the insects living there. It is a guide to selecting, placing, and caring for plants that encourage beneficial insects to do damage control on your behalf.

The objective of my words is to teach you how to design and create a landscape that fosters a diversity of plants and, as a result, a diversity of insects. This diversity does not come as a result of letting your garden go wild, nor does it mean that the insects living there will destroy your plants. To the contrary, insectary gardens are beautiful places filled with healthy, productive plants. They should be a part of every landscape, no matter where you live. Here you will find designs for creating a "good bug" garden of your own—designs suited to suburban lots, city gardens, market farms, and rural backyards.

In this book you will also find interviews with entomologists from across the United States. You'll learn about fascinating research on everything from invasive exotic pests and lost ladybugs to beetle banks and farmscaping. In interviewing these entomologists, I was humbled again and again by the complexities of the workings of the insect world. I continue to have much to learn about the topic and suspect that will be the case for the rest of my life, no matter how much research I do. The scope of the insect world is both infinite and breathtaking. And so, with that in mind, I would like to make a few confessions.

CONFESSION 1 **I used to spray a lot of pesticides.** And I did it without any personal protection or a single thought about the possibility of any negative effects on me or the environment. At age twenty-two, working as a landscaper, I was standing one day on a 6-foot ladder spraying a client's ornamental plum tree for Japanese beetles. The wind

Introducing beneficial insect-friendly plants to your garden not only creates a feast for the eyes, it also creates a feast for all the creatures living there. A well-designed insectary border helps maintain a critical balance between the "good" and the "bad" bugs living in your landscape.

was blowing in my face, and I could taste and smell the chemicals hitting my skin. It didn't bother me one bit. As we were driving back to the company's crew shed that afternoon, my coworker implored me to tell our boss to get me a respirator and some chemical-resistant gloves. In a surprisingly honest and emotional discussion, he told me that his wife, a fellow horticulturist, was having some health problems and her doctor had attributed them to her repeated chemical exposure. He said he didn't want it to happen to me. It got me thinking, and I had my requested respirator and gloves a week later.

CONFESSION 2   **I am a former bug hater.** Eventually I went on to start my own business as a professional gardener. It was my job to make sure forty different gardens looked their best, each and every day. Since my crew and I visited each garden only once per week, anytime I saw a bug, I saw the potential for a less-than-perfect garden and a disappointed client. Insects were nefarious. I carried an arsenal in the car and brought out the pump sprayer whenever I deemed it necessary. Five years after starting my business, I began to turn more to organic products at the prodding of one particular client. Then I hired someone who really set me straight. She taught me much about the dangers of chemical pesticides while we worked side by side in other people's vegetable patches and perennial beds.

I started learning and experimenting and gathering more and more information about what it really means to be an organic gardener.

CONFESSION 3   **I was late in making the connection between good bugs and organic practices.** I thought being organic just meant using different pesticides—ones based on natural ingredients. I certainly didn't think it meant actually encouraging the presence of insects in the garden. Eventually, of course, I learned the importance of beneficial insects, and a few years later I came to the realization that it isn't just the beneficial insects that are desirable but also the pests, for without the latter the beneficial species cannot survive. I developed a true appreciation of the insect world when I wrote my third book, *Good Bug Bad Bug: Who's Who, What They Do, and How to Manage Them Organically*, in 2008. The book is designed as a field guide to identifying common garden pests and beneficials. What is missing from that book, however, is exactly what you'll find in this one: all the tools and information you need to create a garden to protect and balance them both.

CONFESSION 4   **I am not an entomologist.** I didn't really come to appreciate insects (let alone want to make them my profession) until my career as a horticulturist was well under way. But I will say, now that I have dedicated so many hours to learning about insects,

I think I may have missed my calling. I had the great fortune of interviewing many entomologists as I wrote this book, and I am completely and unabashedly fascinated by them (both the insects and the entomologists!). Reading armloads of research papers concerning beneficial insects has served as a healthy reminder that I'm no expert. Not like these folks, at any rate. They are conducting some amazing explorations into the insect world, and what they are discovering is knock-your-socks-off stuff. In writing this book, I relied on them heavily for their expertise and research. So no, I'm not an entomologist but rather an incredibly interested horticulturist who happens to be very keen on the insect world.

CONFESSION 5 I don't like plants as much as I used to. I'm probably going to be shunned for saying this, but to me plants have become static. The insect world, though, is in a constant state of motion. Yes, sometimes insects seem to be villainous scoundrels, but mostly they are just living, breathing beings with a job to do. Before learning about the importance of insects in the garden, my goal was to protect my plants at all costs by wiping out any and all insects that might bring harm; my goal now is to protect my insects, both good and bad, because I have learned what an amazing and indispensable responsibility these tiny creatures have. Today I can say, without a doubt, that I like my insects more than my plants.

CONFESSION 6 I now garden for someone else instead of just for me. I used to go to the nursery and buy a plant because I liked the flower color or I thought it would look good next to my patio or I needed color in September or I liked the plant's texture or form or whatever. Every plant I bought, I bought for me and me alone. But now I know how a beautiful garden lives in harmony with billions of insects. I choose plants for them; I garden for them as much as I do for myself. Because I know that without insects, the world wouldn't be. Without us, however . . . well, who would notice?

all about beneficials

who they are, how they work, and what they eat

Insect-friendly gardens like this one are beautiful places filled with a diversity of plants that are capable of supporting insects of all kinds. They help foster a healthy balance between troublesome pests and the good bugs that help to control them.

"These small creatures are within a few inches of our feet, wherever we go on land—but often, they're disregarded. We would do very well to remember them."

—David Attenborough, *Life in the Undergrowth*

Slug sex is interesting stuff. It's slimy, dangerous, and utterly captivating. It's also how I came to appreciate the insect world. Okay, so officially speaking, slugs aren't insects; they're mollusks. But as I sat on the sofa in 2005 watching the BBC documentary *Life in the Undergrowth*, I couldn't help but be grossly enthralled. The filmmakers had captured the precarious nocturnal dance of two hermaphroditic leopard slugs hanging from a tree by a 2-foot-long

Sure, this seven-spotted ladybug (*Coccinella septempunctata*) looks pretty, but don't be fooled. Each adult is capable of consuming several dozen aphids per day.

thread of viscous slime. It was filmed in high def—making it one of the most uncomfortable and entrancing scenes I have ever witnessed. They dangled there, their iridescent blue "parts" intertwined, loving each other as only two slugs can. The narrator, David Attenborough, spoke of the process as if he were addressing a fifth-grade health class. His words were scientific, matter-of-fact, and yet also electric. The scene was poetic, and in a disturbing kind of way, it was also beautiful (those iridescent blue parts come to a literal full flowerlike bloom before the slugs disen-

gage and fall to the ground). As I watched the rest of that program, and then the remainder of the series, I had an epiphany: there's a lot of remarkable stuff happening out there in my garden. I also suddenly realized my own ignorance.

coming to appreciate insects

As a horticulture major in college, I was required to take only one entomology class. I learned a lot of interesting things about insects, for sure, much of which I will likely never come to use in my career. (Clearly, I'm disappointed that we never covered slug sex, as my professional path might have steered in a different direction had I known then what I know now.) Of greatest significance to me were the weeks we studied agricultural pests. Learning how to distinguish a beetle from a true bug, or a fly from a wasp—now *that* was the kind of information a horticulturist could use. We learned about insect morphology, insect biology, and insect taxonomy. We also learned a lot about what to spray on them to make them disappear. So much for appreciating the insect world.

In the horticulture industry back then, bugs were the bad guys and nothing more. The malicious little thugs were hell-bent on ruining our crops and destroying our livelihood. We were taught to do whatever was necessary to protect our poinsettias, mums, and cyclamen. We never learned a lick about beneficial insects. I was out of college and in my mid-twenties working in public horticulture before I learned that ladybugs are primarily meat eaters. Now kids learn that in the fourth grade. See what I mean about my own ignorance? At least I had an entomology course—many gardeners don't even have that. What they do have is a handful of gardening books, product marketing ploys, the Internet, and a lot of watch-and-learn lessons from Mom and Grandpa.

My guess is that many of us began to learn about gardening (including its insect cohorts) from someone we love. "Dad put Sevin on his cabbage to get rid of the cabbage worms, so that's what I should do, too." We can't help it—actions speak louder than words. Or worse still, the extent of our education about insects comes from a TV commercial with animated six-legged minions munching on leaves and fruits and houses. I would run for the spray can, too, if I didn't know any better. Until recently, the practice of gardening didn't involve insects, other than to understand their role as pollinators and wipe any of the pesty types into oblivion. That's precisely why the slug sex scene was so poignant to me. How could these greasy creatures I had poured salt on, drowned in beer, and poisoned with baits be a part of something so astonishing? Was there other stuff happening out there that could so readily amaze me?

I was an organic gardener by then and knew the value of the good bugs in my landscape, but the epiphany wasn't about that. It was about how I suddenly *needed* to start paying closer attention to all the life in my own undergrowth. Instead of watching it on TV, I began to acknowledge the incredibly fascinating insects living right outside my backdoor. In the years subsequent to my slug-sex revelation, I did a whole lot of reading and research, and I learned that each and every insect in my garden has a story just as enthralling as those slugs (though their reproductive habits may not be quite as hazardous). I quickly came to appreciate the charisma of the insect world, and its presence revealed to me that there's far more to my garden than just the plant kingdom.

classifying bugs

Some 80 percent of the world's animals are insects, most of which have yet to be identified. There are somewhere between two and twenty million insect species on the planet, with a mere one million of them having already been named. Calculations of exact insect numbers are impossible to make, but educated approximations of the total insect population translate to roughly two hundred million insects for each living human. That's a whole bunch of bugs.

All these creatures are in the kingdom Animalia and the phylum Arthropoda (the arthropods). They have segmented bodies, an exoskeleton, and jointed appendages. Arthropods include insects, spiders, mites, ticks, millipedes, centipedes, and others—all of which we commonly refer to as bugs. The arthropods are then further divided into classes (Insecta for the insects, Arachnida for the spiders, and so on) and subsequently into orders.

To get technical about the whole thing, many creatures we call bugs aren't actually bugs at all. *True* bugs are in the class Insecta, order Hemiptera, and are quite separate from beetles, flies, ants, and cockroaches. True bugs include insects like stink bugs, squash bugs, soldier bugs, and assassin bugs. For simplicity's sake, we gardeners often use the term *insect* or *bug* to refer to any arthropod we find in the landscape, so I will do the same throughout this book.

The seven-spotted ladybug, like all living creatures, can be classified into a series of categories from very general to very specific and labeled with a genus and species name.

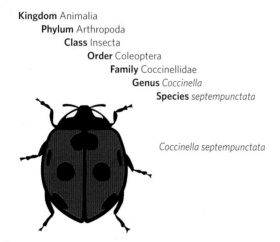

Kingdom Animalia
Phylum Arthropoda
Class Insecta
Order Coleoptera
Family Coccinellidae
Genus *Coccinella*
Species *septempunctata*

Coccinella septempunctata

what bugs do

All these small creatures, even the seemingly vile and destructive ones (those lucky little leopard slugs, for example), serve a purpose. They may be pollinators, decomposers, predators,

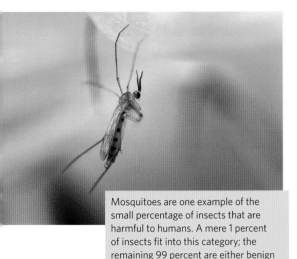

Mosquitoes are one example of the small percentage of insects that are harmful to humans. A mere 1 percent of insects fit into this category; the remaining 99 percent are either benign or beneficial.

The remaining 99 percent of insects are either benign or beneficial. Benign insects are very good at going about their business without harming our crops or us. And beneficial insects are, in fact, doing some type of good in the landscape. Insects can be beneficial for several reasons. First, they can be pollinators. We all know how important quality pollination is to a farm or garden. The world, after all, cannot function without it. Most of us can readily recognize common pollinators like honeybees and butterflies, but there are hundreds of thousands of other pollinator species in this world: beetles, moths, wasps, ants, flies, bats, and birds. Not to mention the more than thirty-five hundred species of native bees in the United States whose pollination work sadly and undeservedly plays second string to that of the imported European honeybee.

or food for someone higher up in the food chain. We are utterly dependent on them to process and decompose organic wastes—without insects we'd be up to our necks in dead stuff and poop—and we use them to produce products like silk, wax, honey, shellac, and certain medicines. Insects are even used to make the natural red food coloring called carmine or cochineal present in many red candies, yogurts, juice drinks, and cosmetics (yes, the red in your rouge may be from dead bugs . . . sorry). We need insects for all sorts of things, and we certainly need them in the garden.

It might surprise you to know that a mere 1 percent of the insects we come across in our lives are actually harmful. These are the creatures that consume our plants, introduce disease, bite our flesh, feed on our pets, and cause economic, aesthetic, or medical damage. These are the bugs that tend to attract our attention, and as a result they get all the press—most of it negative.

European honeybees like this one aren't the only insects that pollinate our crops. There are more than 3500 species of native bees in the United States alone, and hundreds of thousands of other pollinator species around the world.

Fifteen billion dollars worth of food needs to be pollinated by some little creature each and every year in the United States alone. The worth of pollinators is undeniable.

But there is another group of insects that is equally valuable to gardeners. The significance of their work is less recognizable—in part because the results are less tangible to us as the work takes place on a scale far smaller than our own. It's hard to notice what you don't see. And it's even harder to see what you don't know is there in the first place. The insects I'm referring to are commonly called beneficial insects, natural enemies, predatory insects, or even just plain old "good bugs." They are traipsing about our yards and gardens eating and parasitizing many different pests and generally doing a fabulous job of keeping their little world in order. And they are doing it in near silence. Scientifically speaking, they are entomophagous insects, meaning they are insects that eat other insects. A single ladybug—probably the most illustrious beneficial predatory insect—can consume up to five thousand aphids during its lifetime, and a single minute pirate bug—probably the *least* illustrious predatory beneficial—eats about thirty pests per day; and there are thousands of other insect species that do the same.

All these tiny insects are a vital part of your garden. Their inherent intent, of course, is not to help you control pests but rather to survive and reproduce. Isn't it nice, however, that your garden reaps the benefits of their consumptive and reproductive needs? Beneficial insects are waging a war of sorts against garden pests, unintended on their part but advantageous to the garden on so many levels. For too many years these insects have completed their work anonymously. Learning to recognize these natural enemies and encouraging ample populations of them results in a clear win-win situation for both the insect and the gardener.

the garden ecosystem

When we do start paying attention to all the insect life in our garden, as I did after my slug-

Though you might not see them, beneficial insects like this minute pirate bug are hard at work in your landscape, consuming pest insects and helping to maintain a natural balance.

love moment, all anonymity is eliminated and it becomes hard not to appreciate their work. It's a shame, really, that we focus so much on the so-called bad bugs, spending hours and dollars battling them. If we could all manage to switch our focus to encouraging the good bugs, we would allow our gardens to return to a natural balance, giving the control of the garden back to the insect world. But instead, we step in with some sort of pest control that often ends up killing more natural enemies than it does pests, throwing any semblance of natural balance off kilter and creating more problems than we had in the first place. In order to understand why messing with that natural balance has such a negative impact in the garden, we first need to appreciate the garden as an active ecosystem rather than the controlled environment we think it should be.

An ecosystem, in essence, is a community of organisms functioning hand in hand with their environment and each other to exchange energy and create a nutritional cycle. Insects are innately connected to each and every activity occurring in the ecosystem of your garden. A garden simply cannot exist without the actions of the incredible diversity of insects living there. Plants are unable to survive without them. This book focuses on the massive number of links in the garden's ecosystem involving beneficial insects, but we also need to remember how clearly and utterly dependent those links are on the other activities

Predaceous ladybugs are hard at work here creating another generation as they clean up an aphid-infested shrub. Applying a pesticide to this plant to wipe out the aphids would also harm the ladybugs and instantly upset the natural balance.

Each and every plant within the ecosystem of a garden is dependent on numerous insects to survive. Here a honeybee serves to pollinate a Shasta daisy, while a predaceous lacewing larva helps protect it from pest insects.

of every plant, creature, and human there. The garden's web of life is full of small, fragile chains of actions and consequences. Each thread is a living system in and of itself, functioning as a part of the whole. The intricate relationships among plant, pest, and predator form innumerable connections in the web and have great value.

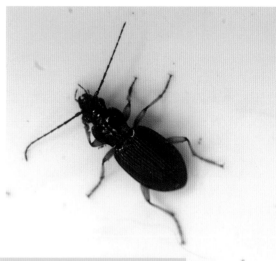

This ground beetle is an example of a secondary consumer in a tritrophic system. It is a true predator capable of capturing and consuming prey.

of predators and prey

The living system in which beneficial insects play such a vital role is tritrophic—meaning it involves three layers of consumption (*tri*, three; *trophic*, eating). At the first trophic level is a plant, which we all learned in grade school is capable of making its own food. For this example, let's use a common hosta as our first trophic level. The second level, known as the primary consumer, then feeds on the hosta. The primary consumer in this tritrophic system is a phytophage, an herbivore feeding on plant tissue. Phytophages feed by chewing leaves, mining leaf tissue, sucking plant sap, boring into wood, or eating seeds or fruits. About half of all known insects are phytophagous. Since it's awfully good at leaf munching, we'll make one of the young hermaphroditic progeny of those two loving leopard slugs the primary consumer (as you probably already know, land mollusks are phytophagous too). Then, on the third-tier trophic level is our secondary consumer, the

predator whose role is to eat the herbivore. Here our secondary consumer is the ground beetle that captures and consumes the immature slug. The guys at the top of this system, the secondary consumers, are the predators. The primary consumers, the phytophagous guys, are the prey.

Before we get into the details of the interplay between predator and prey, I think a further definition of exactly who plays the role of predator is warranted. In the preceding example, the ground beetle is a true predator. He kills and eats the young leopard slug directly (and not necessarily in that order). There are two other groups of organisms that can serve as secondary consumers: parasites and parasitoids.

• A parasite is an organism that spends one or more parts of its life cycle inside of, or

Parasitoids are among the most abundant categories of animals on the planet. A parasitoidal wasp in the genus *Cotesia* has used this tobacco hornworm as a host for its young. The larval wasps consume the caterpillar's innards and emerge through its skin. Within their silken cocoons, they pupate into adults.

attached to, another creature in a nonmutual relationship. A parasite uses its host to obtain nutrition, protection, and, in some cases, progeny dispersal. Often the host's health is diminished, but it survives. It certainly does not benefit the parasite to kill its host.

• A parasitoid, on the other hand, does kill its host, initially using it for the same purposes as a parasite but ultimately bringing death. Parasitoidal insects parasitize their prey by laying eggs inside of, or on, the prey

insect or its eggs. The resulting offspring spend the early developmental stages of their life within, or attached to, their host. Eventually the host dies and the fully mature parasitoid lives independent of a host for the remainder of its life cycle.

In the workings of the garden, parasitic insects don't play a conspicuous role. Yes, you may get a mosquito bite while out in the garden or have a tick latch onto your flesh or, God forbid, wind up with fleas, but other than that, true parasites aren't often noticed by gardeners. A healthy garden, however, is absolutely teeming with parasitoids. Parasitoids are among the most abundant categories of animals on the planet, with about 150,000 described species and many more yet to be named. This population consists mostly of parasitoidal wasp and fly species. Adult female parasitoids find host insects (you'll find out how later) and lay their eggs on or inside of them. These parasitoids are not dangerous to humans or other mammals as they can't sting, nor do they ever use us as hosts. Though they are not in fact true predators, when I use the term *predator* within this text I am also including these parasitoids; after all, their role and importance as secondary consumers in this tritrophic system is enormous.

In addition to these thousands of species of parasitoids are thousands of species of true predatory insects, and each and every one of them eliminates scores of herbivorous insects every day by either having them for lunch or using them as hosts to feed and house their young. The biological system that describes the influence and interplay between the population of prey and their predators is known as the cycle of predator and prey.

Occurring to some extent in nearly every ecosystem on the planet, the cycle of predator and prey is a sequence of events that unless disturbed by outside forces will happen over and over again. In the garden, the predator–prey cycle we are concerned with is the one in which various species of insects fill both roles, but the cycle can be translated to other animals as well—field mice and owls, rabbits and bobcats, minnows and bass.

Among insects, the essence of the predator–prey cycle is this: the prey insect arrives and begins to feed on the plant, and then it increases its reproduction rates and the population increases. As this happens, predators take notice and begin to show up. They find

Appreciating the natural cycle of predator and prey means recognizing that there is a place for pest insects in the landscape. Because the population of predators always lags behind that of prey, gardeners shouldn't panic when pests are discovered. Instead, wait and watch for signs of arriving predators and parasitoids.

plenty of prey available and begin, themselves, to reproduce at a more rapid rate. As these young predators develop and begin to consume prey, the prey population begins to drop. Soon after it does, so does the number of predators.

It's important to see that the population of predators always lags behind that of the prey (this is particularly true if a parasitoid is involved, as their lag time is actually a generation or two behind their host prey). If you put it on paper, it looks much like two undulating, wavy lines with the one representing the predators always hitting its peak slightly after the one representing the prey. In an undisturbed cycle, neither the population of predators nor that of prey will ever hit zero. This means that in order to sustain a healthy population of predators in the garden, one always has to have prey available.

and it matters because . . .

What does this cycle mean to a gardener or farmer? Well, all too often we take notice of a population of naughty pest insects (the prey) when their numbers hit the high point in the cycle. In the case of a pest outbreak, this also happens to be about the same time there are enough prey insects present to start luring in the beneficials. We do something to get rid of the pests just when our little natural army is beginning to work their magic. Whether we choose to eradicate the pests with a synthetic

Watching a population of pests for signs of beneficials always pays off. Here, the same population of aphids noted in the previous photo is now being visited by a species of parasitoidal wasp that will use them as hosts for her young.

or a natural pesticide, we are inserting ourselves into the predator–prey cycle. It's a place where, more often than not, we don't belong. The biggest lesson here is to understand this natural cycle and be willing to take yourself out of it when the time comes.

Instead of taking immediate action against pests, when you come across a population of them, get out your hand lens or magnifying glass (you do have one, don't you?) and check out the situation. As you look at your pests, look for signs of beneficials. Your ability to identify them and understand how they work means you can quite literally watch them do their stuff. You'll be amazed. And remember that within the predator–prey cycle, the predators may take a few days or weeks to arrive on the scene. Give them some time; they'll be there.

Now, just so you don't think I'm completely high on slug love, I am going to point out that there are certainly situations where natural enemies aren't going to be able to get a grip on pest numbers. The contained environments of a greenhouse or your home are two good examples. Houseplants and greenhouse plants can see tremendous pest outbreaks because of the complete lack of natural enemies indoors (though some greenhouses do intentionally introduce beneficial insect species through regular releases). Most importantly, natural enemies may be unable to bring balance when the pest is an exotic species that was imported—accidentally or intentionally—from another region or continent. These insects often don't have any natural enemies in their new territory and as a result are tougher to keep in check. In these situations where there is no predator for the predator–prey cycle, we sometimes have to step in. Our world is facing many challenges regarding the pressures of exotic invasive pests.

refraining from interference in the predator–prey cycle

A few years ago I had the opportunity to witness the marvels of the predator–prey cycle on a grand scale in my own backyard. Though I know it's happening out there on a daily basis, for the first time I got to watch it all unfold. One day I was outside with my son when I noticed the perennials in my shade garden were smothered in sooty mold—a number of species of gray fungi that lend the appearance of a layer of grime. Sooty mold grows on honeydew, and honeydew is the sweet, sticky excrement of various soft-bodied insects. The presence of that coating of sooty mold led me to believe that the tulip poplar tree towering fifty feet above the garden had an issue. Often when trees are plagued by soft-bodied insects, their honeydew coats not only the tree's own foliage but also everything underneath its canopy, and a film of sooty mold is soon to follow. I immediately wanted to know what was going on with the tree; if something happens to this tree and it bites the dust, my shade garden becomes a sun garden, my patio turns into an oven, privacy on that side of the house goes bye-bye, and frankly, I'm just going to be really, really sad. And so the investigation began.

Standing on the swing set, one foot in the belt swing and the other extended behind me for balance, I grasped one of the low-hanging branches. (The neighbors, by the way, would not find this type of backyard behavior the least bit unusual for me.) Holding tight, I jumped off the swing and pulled the branch to eye level. And there on the flip side of each and every leaf were hundreds of pale green aphids in various stages of development. I went for the ladder to examine another branch: same thing—hundreds and hundreds of aphids on every single leaf. What should

the destructive power of exotic invasive insects

Based on an interview with Joseph Patt, PhD, a research entomologist for the United States Department of Agriculture (USDA) Agricultural Research Service, Fort Pierce, Florida

YOU CAN DO EVERYTHING possible to encourage a healthy population of beneficial insects, but when a pest is an introduced exotic species, native natural enemies are seldom able to come to the rescue. Introduced insect species rarely have natural predators or parasitoids in their new environment. "Exotic invasive pests, either plant or animal, pose one of the greatest threats and challenges in this century," says Joseph Patt. "They will continue to be a challenge due to global trade, the movement of people and goods, and the increasing lack of knowledge about natural history in the general population."

Patt explains that exotic invasive insects can be grouped into two categories. The first group of insects consists of those that simply feed on native host plants wherever they have been introduced. The other category includes insects that serve as vectors for pathogenic organisms; in this case not only does the feeding insect cause damage, but so too does the pathogen it introduces. The focus of Patt's research is in the latter category. The ⅛ inch-long Asian citrus psyllid does little damage itself, but the bacterium it transmits causes a devastating disease known as citrus greening or huanglongbing (HLB), the Chinese word meaning "yellow dragon disease."

The bacterium transmitted by the Asian citrus psyllid is like HIV in that once it gets into a host, the host can remain asymptomatic—so that it's impossible to tell that the tree has been infected—for many years. Once the symptoms do appear, the tree dies within one or two years. More than 300,000 acres of orange groves in

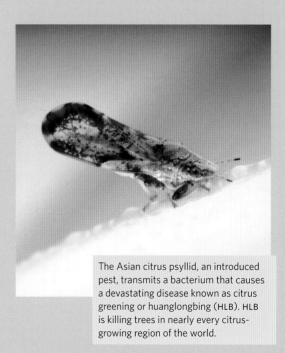

The Asian citrus psyllid, an introduced pest, transmits a bacterium that causes a devastating disease known as citrus greening or huanglongbing (HLB). HLB is killing trees in nearly every citrus-growing region of the world.

Florida have had to be destroyed since 2005 to prevent the spread of HLB infection, and the Asian citrus psyllid has now spread to Texas, California, Georgia, South Carolina, Louisiana, and other citrus-growing states. HLB is also wiping out trees in every citrus-growing region of the world except for Australia and the Mediterranean, though Patt suspects it's just a matter of time until it finds its way to these places as well. "We are in a situation where just one psyllid can kill a tree," says Patt. "How do we save our citrus?"

The destructive power of introduced pests is a global issue. European pests have traveled to Asia; North American pests have arrived in Argentina; Asian insects have invaded the Hawaiian Islands. As Patt and other researchers investigate treatments and controls for introduced pest species, the challenges they face are tremendous. When an exotic pest insect arrives on the scene, there are few, if any, natural enemies to control it and no predator–prey cycle. Parasitoids and predators first have to recognize the foreign insect as food, but they are unfamiliar with the taste, smell, and activities of that particular insect. Patt thinks it's more likely for a microbial attack to limit pest numbers—as happened with gypsy moths—before native arthropods find them appetizing. It *is* possible for a predatory insect to eventually take an interest in the exotic pest as a food source, but first the predator or parasitoid has to mutate a number of times over several generations.

Instead of relying on native predators and parasitoids to control exotic pests, scientists often seek out predators and parasitoids in the pest's native environment and consider releasing them in the pest's new range. Many factors are taken into account and both state and federal agencies are involved before the release of a foreign biological control agent so that it doesn't affect any native insects. Generalist predators—like the multicolored Asian lady beetle, whose overwintering habits have become a bit of a nuisance since its release in the 1900s to control tree pests—are no longer released. The USDA only looks at introducing very specific predators and parasitoids to control exotic pests.

Patt says releasing nonnative predators is a difficult issue and he doesn't know the answer, giving the example of the hemlock woolly adelgid, an introduced pest that kills hemlock trees and as a result wipes out the entire ecosystem where these trees grow. "Scientists ask themselves: Do we release some beetle from China that may secondarily feed on a few native adelgid species while it feeds on the woolly adelgid, or do we let that whole ecosystem collapse?" explains Patt. In the case of the Asian citrus psyllid, the USDA is testing a parasitic wasp from Asia on every single native psyllid in California to be sure it doesn't affect them, and scientists there are also looking at using a native fungus against the psyllids. Other scientists are looking at creating a genetically modified citrus that's distasteful to the insects.

Though the adult moth's face might look cute and fuzzy, gypsy moth caterpillars are responsible for extensive damage to forests across North America. Originally introduced to Massachusetts in the mid-1800s, the moths are now being controlled by several pathogens as well as by various introduced predators and parasitoids.

The Asian citrus psyllid is but one of hundreds of introduced exotic pests around the world; according to the Center for Invasive Species and Ecosystem Health, there are more than 470 invasive insect species in North America alone. The list includes nasties like Japanese beetles, Asian longhorn beetles, emerald ash borers, Mediterranean fruit flies, gypsy moths, and plum curculios. It's estimated that in the United States, a quarter of the agricultural gross national product is lost each year as a result of damage by exotic pests and the costs associated with controlling them. "It's a sad state of affairs," says Patt. "We don't decide this as individuals. Our society has to decide what to do because it isn't going away. People don't think about the effects of moving plant material from one area to another. This is like a tidal wave."

I do? Call a tree company for an application of horticultural oil or an in-ground injection of some synthetic something-or-another that would surely *not* be organic? Save the tree, my gut said, and do it now! Thanks to those TV commercials with the munching minions, in many homeowners' minds one bug equals a pest problem, so here was a situation that very well might send a homeowner over the edge and straight for the chainsaw. I quite literally had to tell myself that I am not an impulsive gardener and I know better. Calm down and stay straight and use this plague as an opportunity to learn something, I told myself.

I knew what to do. Watch the whole situation carefully. Give the good guys some time to do their stuff. I promised myself two weeks of observation from my swing set perch before I took any action at all. At first I checked every other day. No change for nearly a week, just a whole lot of aphids. Then, because we went away for a long weekend, I skipped a few days. On Monday afternoon, I brought the branch down to my eyes and saw what I was hoping for. The back of every leaf now housed not just a colony of aphids but also a single ladybug in some stage of its life cycle—larva, pupa, or adult. I ran for the camera and took several dozen shots of carefully arranged leaves with both predator and prey traipsing about. The image you see here is one of those.

On the third day past my promised two-week observation period, my visual

When aphids erupted on my tulip poplar a few years ago, I watched carefully. Within two weeks, I had discovered numerous species of ladybugs preying on the aphids. And a few days after that, my pest problem was gone.

check revealed nothing but bare-naked leaves. I found no more aphids or ladybugs on that particular branch, just beautiful, green leaves. Had I, or a hired tree care company, stepped in, the whole cycle would have been shut down and all those ladybugs would have never come to be. The take-home from a moment like this is that fighting the flow of nature by involving yourself in a process where you don't belong seldom brings long-term positive results. A quick fix may seem the best answer, but clearly it isn't. Nature has been fixing stuff slowly for millennia. I still get excited about the whole thing, and part of me wants it to happen all over again just so I can invite everyone I know over to see how amazing it is.

creating a safe place for beneficials to live

It may seem that cutting yourself out of the predator–prey cycle and having enough prey around would be enough to keep your beneficial insects happy. This isn't the case. We also have to create the right environment for them. First and foremost, that environment needs to be pesticide free—and not just free of chemical pesticides, either. Ideally, all backyard pesticide use should stop (except, perhaps, in cases of introduced exotic pest outbreaks where the risk of death to an entire population of plants is extremely high—as is the case

with the emerald ash borer, for example).

Here's why. Let's start with what happens when a synthetic chemical is applied to a perceived pest outbreak. Most of the pest insects are killed, yes, but some survive. Those that do are more likely to be resistant to that particular pesticide. They go on to breed and pass that trait along to their young. Over time and several generations, the localized population of that pest becomes resistant to that pesticide. Increasing the rate of resistance further is the gardener or farmer who is continuing to use the same pesticide every time more of those pests are spotted.

Spider mites are notorious for developing resistance to pesticides. To make matters worse, any pesticides used against them also wipe out their many natural enemies. Without these natural enemies to keep the mite numbers in check, their population rebounds quickly and secondary pest outbreaks are more likely.

The other major factor that comes into play was touched upon earlier: many beneficial insects are just as, if not more, susceptible to the effects of the pesticides. Pesticide exposure is detrimental to the health of beneficials in several ways. Not only do they come into direct physical contact with sprays, but they are also exposed through their consumption of contaminated prey. In essence, you wipe the beneficials out too, so any pests that do survive have both an increased resistance to the pesticide and no remaining natural enemies. They often rebound with a vengeance.

Secondary pest outbreaks are also more likely in this situation. This happens when the population of a completely different pest species balloons because they too have no remaining natural enemies to keep them in check. Disrupting the population of beneficial insects through the use of chemical pesticides is an open invitation for pests to chow down on your rutabagas.

Though the resistance factor isn't quite as great with many natural pesticides, the effects on beneficial insect populations can be. Many organic and natural pesticides come with label warnings not to apply when bees or other beneficial insects are present. But how do you know whether beneficials are present? Yes, you may be able to spot a ladybug, but not a single gardener I know can tell if a caterpillar, an aphid, or some other bad guy is serving as host to the larva of some parasitoidal wasp

until the latter stages of the process. Spraying a seemingly safe product like horticultural oil on a colony of aphids results in plenty of collateral damage. You kill the aphids and also the larval wasps inside. You may also unintentionally smother ladybug eggs tucked underneath a nearby leaf, coat a predatory fly larva scouting for an aphid lunch on a plant stem, or suffocate tiny predatory bugs scuttling on the soil surface beneath the plant. All that collateral damage is simply not worth it.

And then, of course, there's the point that even if you don't directly harm any beneficial

Applications of even seemingly safe pesticides like horticultural oil can cause a lot of collateral damage. Ladybug eggs clinging to a leaf underside are easily smothered by the oil.

At some point in their life cycle, nearly all beneficial insects, including this predatory soldier beetle, need to consume pollen and nectar to survive and reproduce. In turn, these insects transfer pollen from flower to flower as they go.

species, you're taking away their buffet, their reason to stick around and maintain balance. Fewer pests might seem like a good thing, but in reality, fewer pests means fewer beneficials—a situation that almost always leads to an increased risk of major pest outbreaks.

providing the protein and carbohydrates an insect needs

As you can see, pesticide-free habitat is an absolute necessity for natural enemies. The reasons why such an environment is so important, though, go far beyond an insect's need for a safe haven. The shelter it provides is essential. Natural enemies are, after all, not at the pinnacle of the food chain. They, too, can become a meal for some higher-up. Affording them protection from other predators, like birds, toads, snakes, and, yes, lots and lots of other insects, is part of the function of their habitat. Found here as well are breeding partners, egg-laying sites, places to hunker down for the winter, and three square meals a day (more or less, anyway).

Those meals, of course, are compulsory for an insect's growth and maturation, as well as for its ability to create progeny and live a long, healthy life. But the active and ample populations of prey housed in quality habitat are but a portion of the food necessary for many predators. Nearly all beneficial insects require not only the proteins found in their prey but also the protein in pollen. And at some point in their life cycle, the majority of beneficial insects also need the carbohydrates produced by plants in the form of nectar. They convert these plant-sourced carbohydrates into energy for movement as well as using them to increase their fertility. Some also consume carbohydrates through the ingestion of honeydew (I'm sure many of those ladybugs in my tulip poplar a few years ago were slurping down their share). Nectar and pollen, sourced from a diversity of plants, are in fact essential elements in the nutritional needs of insect predators and parasitoids. As a bonus, while these insects are consuming nectar and pollen, they are also serving as pollinators, transferring pollen among the many flowers they are visiting each and every day.

A gardener wants beneficial insects to dedicate as much of their energy as possible to finding and eliminating plant-eating pests. Ideally, beneficial insects should minimize nectar and pollen foraging so they can spend their energies on finding hosts or lunch. If the prey insect and the nectar are in different locations, beneficials have to spend an awful lot of travel time between the two to fulfill both their reproductive and nutritional needs, something you don't want to encourage. Having all these goodies in one location—your backyard—is exactly what you, and they, want. The goal should be to create a landscape that

Creating a landscape with a diversity of plant-based foods is critical to the fitness of beneficial insects. Doing so minimizes nectar and pollen foraging time and allows the insects to spend their energies on finding prey or hosts.

offers a diversity of plant-based foods to support the performance and vitality of all the insects living there.

keeping beneficial insects in the landscape

Insects, as you already know, are not stationary. They move about the landscape by flying or crawling, scooting or jumping. But except for migrating species, they prefer not to travel far, especially if they don't have to. When their basic needs—food, shelter, water, and reproduction—are being met, there isn't much of a reason to leave. For predatory and parasitoidal insects, if the proper balance of plant-based nutrition and prey insects isn't available, they will leave to find what's missing (a process known as commuting). The larger the distance they have to travel, the smaller the chance of their return. If a predator leaves a pest-plagued area because it needs to access nectar, it is unlikely to return to that place, especially if it finds a new location with both ample amounts of nectar and additional prey. All those ladybugs in my tulip poplar tree were happy there because they had not only plenty of prey available to them but also a garden full of nectar and pollen. Though ladybug larvae primarily consume other insects, the adult beetles of many ladybug species need nectar and pollen to survive and reproduce.

If natural enemies have a nutritionally balanced diet, their rates of parasitism, predation, and reproduction increase. To achieve such a balance, provide ample nectar and pollen sources as well as plenty of available prey via a diverse, pesticide-free garden ecosystem.

Nectar quality also plays a major role in the productivity of many natural enemies. Their foraging activities are affected by the accessibility, quantity, and quality of nectar. A variety of nectar sources increases the life span of many species; for others, nectar and/or pollen is a nutritional necessity before egg laying can occur. Of utmost importance to the gardener is the knowledge that if natural enemies are well fed and their diet is nutritionally balanced, their rates of parasitism, predation, and reproduction go up. This just makes sense; for any living being, proper nutrition comes first.

Much of the intriguing research in today's entomological community underscores the value of designing our gardens with beneficial insects in mind. Sometimes we need the experts to prove it before we are willing to change our own gardening habits. One interesting study found that a species of parasitoidal wasp (we gardeners often call them *parasitic* wasps, which isn't as specific as *parasitoidal* but is far more commonly used, so I'm going to refer to them as parasitic wasps from here on out) released into a cotton field with ample nectar present, fed on that nectar longer and went on to parasitize a higher number of hosts than did females released into a nectarless cotton field. The study found that hungry females were less efficient at finding hosts and that food deprivation affected their longevity and egg production. And there are scores of other studies detailing the same. It's clear that the presence of quality nectar and pollen directly correlates with high parasitism rates and therefore contributes to a better balance of good and bad bugs in our gardens.

It's important to note that nectar foraging is also affected by the presence of certain chemicals in the nectar. When these chemicals are present, foraging insects avoid the nectar entirely and leave. The chemicals in certain pesticides can contaminate nectar and decrease its ability to serve as a food source. Systemic pesticides, in particular, which travel through a plant's entire vascular system, can cause an increased incidence of insect mortality to those insects feeding on the nectar. If I had chosen to inject my tulip poplar's root zone with a systemic pesticide, all the surrounding flowering plants would have absorbed it through their roots as well. Any ladybugs that arrived before the aphids were killed by the pesticide may not have stuck around, or they may have been killed themselves because both their prey source and their nectar source were contaminated. Many other pesticides can also accumulate in floral nectars and greatly influence both the foraging habits and the health of pollinating insects. Garden

environments that best support and encourage a diversity of natural enemies are those that provide shelter, ample prey, and consistent, diverse, and *safe* nectar and pollen sources.

how beneficial insects find their prey

Of the many behaviors beneficial insects perform on a daily basis, finding prey is, to me, the most fascinating. The idea that an insect predator is able to find its minuscule prey in what must seem a vast expanse of jungle is absolutely astonishing to me. How is that ground beetle able to find our young slug? How did all those ladybugs know about the aphids on my tulip poplar? How did those parasitic wasps in the cotton field discover their insect hosts in the first place? How does any insect predator find its prey? In most cases, combinations of visual and olfactory (scent) cues are used to locate prey. Learning is involved too, but we'll get to those astounding details later.

While predators can certainly see their prey and attack it based solely on a visual prompt, it's the nuances of the olfactory cues that make this whole tritrophic system so awe inspiring. Insects and plants have evolved an intricate communication system in the form of chemical signals (called semiochemicals) released into the air. Some of these signals (such as one put out by an insect looking for

This female parasitic wasp uses a set of cues to locate her aphid hosts. The damaged plant releases volatile chemicals into the air that serve to attract the wasp. The plant, in essence, is delivering an SOS in hopes of recruiting predators and parasitoids.

a mate) are species specific while others are capable of crossing kingdoms and allowing plants and insects to message each other. The olfactory cues used by predators to find prey come in the form of volatile chemicals produced by both plants and insects.

Many pest-infested plants emit semiochemicals known as herbivore-induced plant volatiles (HIPV) or green leaf volatiles into the air to lure in the particular species of natural enemy most likely to prey upon the specific pest present on the plant. These scents, which travel anywhere from a few inches to hundreds of yards from their source, are detected by the predator and/or parasitoid and used to locate its prey. Several studies have found that female parasitic wasps are not attracted to aphids alone but rather to the semiochemicals produced by the infested plants. The plant, in essence, is sending out an SOS; it is recruiting predators to come to its aid.

My tulip poplar tree began to release ladybug-luring HIPVs the moment the aphid population began to rise. A corn plant releases a specific HIPV when being attacked by a corn earworm; a lima bean plant sends out an SOS when mites begin to feed; a tomato plant emits an HIPV when a hornworm bites into a leaf. Even more amazingly, the specific semiochemical released by a plant depends upon the exact species of pest attacking it. If a species of pest caterpillar had been attacking my tulip poplar, the tree would have released a different HIPV intended to attract a different predator or parasitoid to the area, and this HIPV would have been specific to that distinct caterpillar species. Several studies have even noted a plant's ability to release particular semiochemicals when a pest deposits eggs on its leaves—semiochemicals intended to attract a species of parasitic wasp that uses insect eggs as hosts. The sophistication of this system is utterly astonishing.

We humans, of course, aren't nasally refined enough to pick up on these olfactory cues, nor do we sport the sensitive antennae of the insect world. The communication system between the plant world and the insect one is a complicated affair. It makes me wonder if we will ever know the extent to which we humans are messing it all up simply through our own ignorance. Does the scent of a dryer sheet on my clothes confuse them? My soap? My shampoo? Such semiochemical interference, of course, would be accidental, but we humans have learned to use HIPVs to influence insect behavior on purpose. The

last chapter of this book contains information on how we use HIPVs to lure predators and parasitoids to a particular area.

Insects too release semiochemicals. Pheremones are a type of semiochemical released by insects to communicate within their particular species, perhaps to attract a mate, to sound an alarm, or to induce feeding behaviors. Natural enemies also produce them to mark their territory and deter competitors. Ladybugs leave behind a semiochemical footprint to indicate their presence to other predators. Predatory mites, too, target prey in areas where fewer competing predators are detected, though this comes about as a result of semiochemicals produced by the prey rather than by the other predators. Regardless, predators know about each other through the presence of semiochemicals, and they make feeding decisions based on them. The intricacy of this system cannot be overstated.

how beneficials learn to see your yard as desirable

To top off all this complexity and put the proverbial icing on the cake, some beneficial insects are also capable of learning, largely in the form of benefiting from a particular signal and then relying on it repeatedly to increase chances of success. Predatory insects use visual and olfactory cues based on their current nutritional needs. The odor of damaged leaves, for example, will lure in a female parasitoid looking to find host insects to parasitize or a true predator looking for a bite of lunch, while the scent of nectar is more likely to lure in an insect in need of nutrition from pollen or nectar. If the scent of vanilla yields more nectar than the scent of honey, they'll return to the vanilla-scented flowers first.

Color also plays a part. If orange flowers repeatedly yield ample nectar, when given a choice the insect will choose orange over other flower colors. The female parasitic wasps in one study were more attracted to the color yellow (the most common flower color) when they were in need of nectar, while their satiated sisters were more attracted to green (the color of the leaves most likely to have host insects present). These insects can make decisions on which cue to follow based on whether they are hungry or looking for someplace to lay eggs.

All of these results were obtained in laboratory tests, but it stands to reason that if an insect is capable of this type of learning in a controlled environment, it has already evolved the ability to do so in its natural surroundings. Negative experiences, too, are learned. For example, if a particular visual or olfactory signal no longer leads to food, insects stop responding to it. Many studies have been done, with more under way, that outline an insect's ability to learn characteristics of its hosts and of nectar sources once it has had contact with

Amazingly, some beneficial insects are capable of learning, mostly in the form of benefiting from a particular cue and then relying on it in the future to increase their chances of foraging success. For example, if yellow flowers, like this sunflower, repeatedly yield more nectar in lab studies, the insects are more likely to head to yellow flowers the next time a color choice is presented.

them. It then uses that information to increase the chances of foraging success in the future.

This all indicates that beneficial insects have the ability to learn to see your yard as one where they can successfully find habitat, prey, pollen, and nectar—that is, of course, if you are willing to make it such a place.

beneficial bug profiles

meet the predators and the parasitoids

beneficial insects are extremely prevalent in a healthy garden. A cotton field in Arkansas, for example, was found to host more than six hundred different species of natural enemies. That could translate to millions of individual predators and parasitoids per acre. And this study took place in a monoculture. Imagine the number of predatory and parasitoidal insects in the mixed habitat of an insectary border! Though one natural enemy species alone might not be able to make a huge impact, collectively their influence on pest numbers is tremendous.

This chapter introduces you to many of the common predators and parasitoids that can be found throughout the temperate

Some 80 percent of the world's animals are insects, and a mere 1 percent of them are classified as harmful. The rest are either benign or beneficial. Insects are at work in all environments, and by creating islands of plant diversity like this one, we can help support countless species of insects.

regions of the United States and Canada. Recognizing these beneficials either by their appearance or by noting the physical evidence of their actions enables you to appreciate them for the work they do on your garden's behalf. If you can't discern a ground beetle from a cockroach or an assassin bug from a squash bug, how will you know who to cheer and who to chide?

In this chapter I've arranged the insects into several broad groupings. There are the true bugs, the true flies, the predatory beetles, the parasitic wasps, the dragon- and damselflies, the lacewings, the mantids, and the arachnids. Within each of these groups, you'll see I've highlighted specific insects based on the important role each of them plays in the biological control of pests in the landscape. The insects within each group are listed alphabetically by their common name.

Within the assemblage of predators and parasitoids I describe are generalists and specialists. Generalist predators do not feed exclusively on any one insect. They attack and consume prey based on what is available to them and whether they are able to capture it. Yes, many generalist predators have preferences and will not eat just *anything*, but generalists tend to feed on a broad range of insect prey species. Specialists, on the other hand, prey on or use as a host only a few closely related species of insects. Many parasitoids are specialists, targeting a single host.

To complicate things further, generalist predator families can include specialist species. For example, among the lacewings, which are considered generalist predators, are a handful of specialist species that target only one type of prey. The same goes for predatory stink bugs, hoverflies, and even members of the ladybug family. As I describe which pests a particular natural enemy family targets, keep in mind that there may be both generalists and specialists involved.

true bugs

Found within the insect order Hemiptera are the true bugs. These insects each have two pairs of overlapping wings, most often with the forewings being hardened at the base and the hind wings being entirely membranous. Nearly all true bugs undergo a simple metamorphosis, passing through three life stages—egg, nymph, and adult—often with the nymphal stage looking much like the adult except without wings and of smaller stature. Another important feature of true bugs is their piercing-sucking mouthpart, used to drain fluids from prey or plants.

• •

Assassin bugs

FAMILY **Reduviidae**

NORTH AMERICAN SPECIES **100+**

If there were a ninja of the insect world, this dude would be it. The aptly named assassin bug is sneaky, swift, vicious, and deadly—and it's no lightweight. Adults can measure 0.5–1.0 inch (13–25 mm) in length, depending on the species. The most commonly encountered assassin bugs are the spined assassin, the masked hunter, wheel bugs, and those within the genus *Zelus*. Some species are brightly colored, but most assassin bugs are brown, green, or black. They have broad bodies, elongated heads, and long, spindly legs. Females lay eggs on plants and the resulting nymphs (with their distinctive swaybacks) pass through several stages before fully maturing. Depending on the species, assassins can overwinter as adults, nymphs, or eggs, enabling them to live for several years.

The assassin's weapon of choice is a sharp, curved, daggeresque mouthpart (called a rostrum) that it keeps tucked under its body until it's time to feed. It uses its enlarged,

This brilliant orange assassin bug (*Pselliopus barberi*) uses its curved mouthpart to kill and consume insect prey.

predators eating predators: intraguild predation

This crab spider has captured a syrphid fly on a peony bud. Both of these insects are predators—the spider for its entire life cycle and the syrphid fly as a larva—so this is an example of intraguild predation (IGP).

MOLECULAR GUT-CONTENT analysis is probably just as fun as it sounds. It is one of the processes that entomologists (and their students) use to discover what insect predators eat. Since you can't ask a bug what it had for a midnight snack, determining its diet is a bit of challenge. Molecular gut-content analysis allows entomologists to find out who is preying on whom by examining the amounts and sources of the DNA found in the digestive system of a predatory insect. What this and other techniques have confirmed in many studies is that predatory insects eat not only their herbivorous prey but also other predatory insects.

When a predator attacks and consumes a competing predator, it's known as intraguild predation (IGP). IGP is a routine occurrence in the ecosystem of the garden and the farm. Two insects that compete for the same prey will readily target each other. A team of entomologists found that more than half the ladybugs collected in a field of soybeans had remnants of other ladybug species in their guts, and many of them had ingested multiple species. IGP influences the distribution and population of both natural enemies and prey. The extent of IGP in the average garden or farm field is tough to gauge because it's dependent on factors ranging from insect population dynamics and life cycles to pesticide use and the presence of semiochemicals.

What we know for sure is that predators attack other predators, and that predators eat prey that are already hosting a parasitoid. I am mentioning all this not to make you crazy with envy for the folks who get to perform molecular gut-content analysis but rather to emphasize the complicated structure of predation. A lot of variability exists in the relationships among predators, parasitoids, and their prey—and between predators and parasitoids.

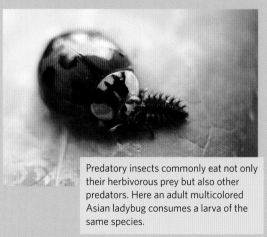

Predatory insects commonly eat not only their herbivorous prey but also other predators. Here an adult multicolored Asian ladybug consumes a larva of the same species.

raptorial front legs to ambush and capture prey, which it then pierces with its "sword" and injects with a lethal toxin, killing the prey within minutes. The same toxin then liquefies the unlucky captive's innards in short order, enabling the assassin to slurp it up and leave nothing but the empty exoskeleton behind.

It might sound a bit gross until you consider just what the assassin bug is having for lunch. Common prey include garden nasties like hornworms, Mexican bean beetles, Colorado potato beetles, leafhoppers, cucumber beetles, aphids, caterpillars of all sorts, and many other insect species. Mind you, this is a generalist predator that isn't overly discriminating and will capture a ladybug or two along the way (intraguild predation at its finest!), but overall it's on the right team, working to control pests in the landscape.

Zelus luridus, like other assassin bugs, is an ambush hunter. It uses a sticky substance produced on its forelegs to further ensnare its captured prey before piercing it with its rostrum.

Assassin bugs are not drawn to any specific landscape plants as they feed exclusively on other insects. However, diverse plantings provide the physical habitat they need as well as ample numbers of prey insects.

Both adult and nymph assassins are covert little buggers and aren't usually encountered by gardeners on a regular basis. At best, you might come across one or two each season.

• •

Big-eyed bugs

FAMILY Lygaeidae, subfamily Geocoridae
NORTH AMERICAN SPECIES 12+ *Geocoris* species

Yes, they are small—measuring a mere 0.375 inch (10 mm) at maturity—but big-eyed bugs are also mighty. Each one is capable of consuming several dozen pests per day, making them among the most valuable natural enemies around. They are also among the most abundant. As generalist predators, they eat a protein-based diet including insect eggs, spider mites, aphids, cabbage worms, caterpillars, flea beetles, leafhoppers, thrips, lygus bug nymphs, corn earworms, whiteflies, and many, many others. One study revealed that big-eyed bugs consume sixty-seven different varieties of insects! These beneficials forage for pests on plants as well as on the soil, making these microhelpers incredibly important to gardeners.

Both the nymphs and adults of this amazing little insect are protein eaters. Slightly oblong with a broad head and distinctive wide-set bulging eyes (which help them spot their prey as well as their predators), the adults have clear wings that overlap and rest on their backs. They are brown, black, or gray in color. Females lay eggs on or near prey clusters to enable the hatching nymphs to find food quickly. Each female can lay up to three hundred eggs in her lifetime. Nymphs look much the same as adults except they're a bit smaller and lack wings. Big-eyed bugs mature from egg to adult in about thirty days.

Though their primary food source is other insects, big-eyed bugs also feed on nectar, sap, and small seeds to sustain themselves when prey are scarce. They spend the winter in garden debris and grassy areas, and emerge in the spring to begin feeding on prey by piercing them with a specialized mouthpart and sucking out the internal organs (not a bad thought when you consider exactly whose guts they're consuming!). I often find big-eyed bugs in my strawberry patch as well as under the skirts of many low-lying garden plants. Several studies have pointed to the value of cover crops such as crimson clover and alfalfa in increasing big-eyed bug populations. It's also important to remember that since these beneficial bugs are capable of surviving on nectar, seeds, and sap, having a diversity of flowering plants around means these predators will already be present if and when a pest outbreak occurs.

Among the most abundant predators, big-eyed bugs consume dozens of different insects. Though they are small, they are very valuable allies. This adult *Geocoris uliginosus* is one of a dozen-plus species occurring in the United States.

The wide-set, bulging eyes of *Geocoris punctipes* help it to spot both prey and predators, and its specialized mouthpart is used to suck out the prey's internal organs.

Damsel bugs

FAMILY **Nabidae**

NORTH AMERICAN SPECIES **40+**

The name *damsel bug* may imply that these creatures are somehow delicate and ladylike, but nothing could be further from the truth. (I'm guessing that the chap who decided upon that name must have really been worked over by some ex-girlfriends.) Much like its cousin the assassin bug, the damsel bug has raptorial front legs. The many potential victims of the damsel bug include insect eggs, aphids, small caterpillars, corn earworms, cabbage worms, corn borers, leafhoppers, larval sawflies, mites, plant bugs, asparagus beetles, Colorado potato beetles, and whatever else it can get its raptorial paws on. To heighten the irony of this common name, damsel bugs use a sharp, swordlike rostrum to stab their insect quarry and suck it dry—hardly ladylike behavior in my book.

This adult damsel bug captures prey with its raptorial front legs. These bugs are small, move quickly, and can be difficult to spot.

This damsel bug nymph has captured a fly and is using its rostrum to retrieve the fly's liquefied innards. Nymphs look much like adults except they are smaller and do not have wings.

Damsel bugs are slender tan insects measuring a mere 0.25–0.35 inch (6–9 mm) in length. They have stiltlike legs and a narrow head and keep their rostrum tucked under their body when it's not being used. Nymphs look much like adults but are smaller and without wings. Some species of damsel bugs are great fliers and have been collected thousands of feet in the air and miles out to sea. Damsel bugs can survive for up to two weeks with no food, but they are so voracious they'll turn to cannibalism before they'll go hungry. Some reports of damsel bugs eating plant tissue do exist, but the behavior seems to be rare. What we do know is that in times of prey or water scarcity, some species of damsel bugs feed on nectar.

Though they move very rapidly, damsels also fall victim to intraguild predation, with a handful of parasitoids using them as hosts. As generalist predators they also take part in

IGP by capturing and consuming other predators. Most damsel bugs overwinter as adults and begin to appear in spring. They shelter in low plants, grasses, and ground covers. My raspberry patch is home to a posse of damsel bugs every year. I find them there nearly every day hanging out on leaf undersides waiting to ambush some unlucky victim.

● ●

Minute pirate bugs

FAMILY **Anthocoridae**

NORTH AMERICAN SPECIES **70+**

Because of their tiny size, minute pirate bugs usually escape notice even though they are among the most common predators in our yards and gardens. Adults measure a mere 0.08–0.2 inch (2–5 mm) in length. They are oval black-and-silver insects with clear wings that overlap under their rigid wing covers and extend slightly beyond their body. The orange to brown, wingless, pear-shaped nymphs are smaller still. Despite their minuscule stature, minute pirate bugs are wicked predators, consuming pests like thrips, spider mites, insect eggs, aphids, small caterpillars, corn earworms, leafhopper nymphs, psyllids, scale crawlers, and whiteflies, to name just a few.

Some seventy species of minute pirate bugs exist across North America, with most species being generalist predators. However, a few specialist species do exist, living largely on one plant species as a result of their specialized feeding habits. *Orius tristicolor* is among the most common species in the West, while *Orius insidious* (also called the insidious flower

Minute pirate bugs, like this *Orius insidious*, are primarily meat eaters. However, they do feed on flower pollen when prey are scarce. Their overlapping clear wings extend slightly beyond their body, creating a distinctive silvery diamond shape.

Because of their very small stature, minute pirate bugs are difficult to see. This one is resting on the back of a dime-sized feverfew blossom waiting for prey. Their needlelike mouthpart ingests the internal fluids of their victim once captured.

plant juices (though never to the detriment of the plant), they are susceptible to systemic insecticide applications. These diminutive predators are often found crawling around the flowering stems of plants as well as leaf undersides where they are stalking their prey. Minute pirate bugs feed by piercing their captured prey with a needlelike mouthpart and ingesting the internal fluids.

Several foreign species of minute plant bugs have been released in North America over the years to control pear psyllids, balsam woolly adelgids, and laurel thrips. Others have been released unintentionally. North American species have also been introduced to other parts of the world.

bug) is a primary species east of the Rockies. Both adults and nymphs are predatory and can consume thirty or more pests per day. As true predators, they are active participants in intraguild predation, consuming and being consumed by other generalist predators.

Minute pirate bugs overwinter as adults, with day length determining when the insects shift into and out of diapause (a physiological state of dormancy akin to hibernation). Adults emerge in spring and begin to feed. Though they are primarily meat eaters, minute pirate bugs also feed on pollen and plant juices when prey are scarce, making early-blooming plants and flowers important to their survival. Females go on to lay eggs in plant tissue. The eggs hatch three to five days later and the nymphs pass through five instars (life stages between molts) before maturing into adults.

Because minute pirate bugs also suck

Predatory stink bugs

FAMILY Pentatomidae, subfamily Asopinae
NORTH AMERICAN SPECIES approximately 35

When someone hears the name *stink bug*, the likely reaction is a crunched up nose, a furrowed brow, and utterance of the phrase "eee-www." Having been subjected to the stench of these creatures on any number of occasions, I don't blame them. With the majority of the 250 species of stink bugs in North America being plant-eating pests (and some of them serious ones at that), it's easy to see why they have such a stinky reputation. The subfamily Asopinae, however, consists of only predatory species. These are the good guy stink bugs.

All stink bugs stink. Even the beneficial species emit a distinct odor when handled or threatened. It is a defense mechanism—and a good one at that. Stink bugs have a broad, shield-shaped body and are fairly large (0.27–0.8 inch, or 7–20mm, depending on the species). They can be brown, gray, green, black, or multicolored with red, orange, pink, or yellow markings. Their eggs are barrel shaped and are laid in groups on plant foliage. Nymphs pass through five instars (life stages between molts) before maturing. The rounded nymphs look very different from adults in coloration and form, and often are gregarious, grouping together to attack prey or feed on plant tissue. Predaceous members of the stink bug family are known to consume common garden pests like caterpillars, Japanese beetles, Mexican bean beetles, Colorado potato beetle, lygus bug nymphs, beetle larvae, bollworms, herbivorous stink bugs, and others. They also will occasionally suck plant juices to supplement their diet and provide needed moisture, though they seldom cause significant damage (unlike their herbivorous cousins).

Probably the most common and important predaceous stink bug is the spined soldier bug. The grayish brown adults have shoulders with sharp points protruding from them. The rounded, wingless nymphs are orange with black markings. Spined soldier bugs, and other predaceous stink bugs, feed by stabbing prey with a knifelike mouthpart and consuming

Anchor stink bugs (*Stiretrus anchorago*), like other predaceous members of the stink bug family, are important predators, consuming a broad range of common garden pests. This one is feeding on an eastern tent caterpillar.

The eggs of the spined soldier bug are downright beautiful—with a shiny metallic exterior, a brilliant blue interior, and a single row of soft spikes encircling the top—but this egg clutch has fallen victim to intraguild predation. A tiny parasitic wasp in the family Platygastridae has inserted her own eggs into them and is now standing guard, protecting them from other predators.

the innards. Spined soldier bugs are large, 0.35–0.55 inch (9–14 mm) long, and feed primarily at night. Nine other predatory species share the genus *Podisus* with the spined soldier bug. There are also several other types of predatory stink bugs, including the two-spotted stink bug, the anchor stink bug, and the handsome members of the genus *Tylospilus*, along with their many relatives. While many predaceous stink bugs are generalist predators, several specialist species also exist.

Predatory and herbaceous stink bugs serve as food for birds, spiders, assassin bugs, and, yes, even other species of predatory stink bugs. In some parts of the world, including Mexico and Southeast Asia, some species of stink bugs also serve as food for humans. They are eaten whole or pounded into a paste and combined with other ingredients for a savory side dish full of protein.

It is very difficult to discern the plant-eating stink bugs from the pest-eating ones. If you are up for it, a careful examination of their rostrum will tell you who is who. Predatory species have a wide, free-moving rostrum attached only where it meets the head, while plant-feeding stink bugs have a narrow rostrum with the entire first segment fused to the underside of the insect's head. Though I have never cared to examine them that carefully myself, one of these days I'm going to, just so I can share the news at cocktail parties. Who wouldn't be interested in that?

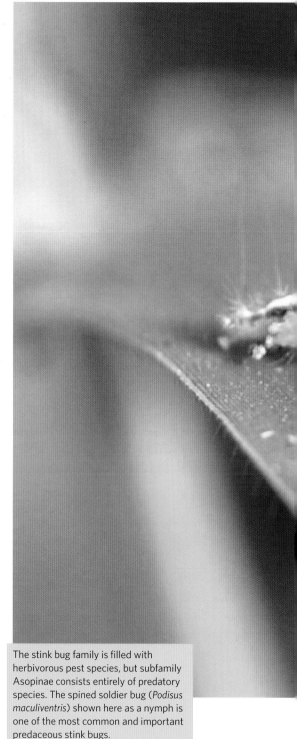

The stink bug family is filled with herbivorous pest species, but subfamily Asopinae consists entirely of predatory species. The spined soldier bug (*Podisus maculiventris*) shown here as a nymph is one of the most common and important predaceous stink bugs.

true flies

The insect order Diptera consists of the true flies, gnats, mosquitoes, and their relatives. All true flies have a single pair of functional wings (*di* = two, *ptera* = wings) and a pair of smaller clublike structures that serve to balance them during flight. True flies pass through a complete metamorphosis with four distinct life stages—egg, larva, pupa, and adult. Larvae, called maggots, lack legs and move through muscle contraction. The small handful of true fly families I describe here are well known for their pest-controlling prowess, either as true predators or, as with the tachinid family, as parasitoids.

Robber flies are distinguished by a long, tapered abdomen and a bristly face and legs. These generalist predators consume many different insects, including lots of common pests. They can grab their prey in midflight or snatch it off foliage or flowers in a split second.

Robber flies

FAMILY **Asilidae**

NORTH AMERICAN SPECIES **1000+**

If you have yet to encounter a robber fly in the garden, consider yourself forewarned. They are bristly, bold, creepy-looking flies that can send even the most stoic gardener diving for the flyswatter. They shouldn't be swatted or otherwise harmed, however, because this large group of predatory flies is super good at eating meat, including Colorado potato beetles, plant bugs, grasshoppers, Japanese beetles, aphids, leafhoppers, and scores of others. Of course, they'll also catch bees, butterflies, spiders, and other good guys upon occasion. As generalist predators, they are not judicious diners.

Watching one of these flies work makes for a pretty remarkable garden moment. In true Dracula fashion, robber flies often nab their prey midflight—snatching them up with their spindly, hairy legs and finding a perch on which to consume them. Robber flies can also seize prey off plants and flowers in a mere instant. Once the tasty morsel has been captured, the fly uses its swordlike mouthpart to inject it with toxic saliva. The enzymes in the saliva liquefy the prey's innards, and the robber fly then slurps them up like a protein shake, leaving only the empty exoskeleton behind.

Robber flies have two wings and can measure up to 1.5 inches (38 mm) in length.

Most species are gray to black in color (though a few species are amazing bee mimics). Their long tapered abdomens, large eyes, and bristly faces and legs make for easy recognition. Working in the garden, I am apt to bump into one or two each day, often with some unfortunate victim in their grasp. They much prefer open, sunny spaces; I most frequently find them in the vegetable garden or perennial borders.

In addition to their unique physical features and semi-repulsive eating habits, robber flies have a fascinating life cycle. Mating occurs much the same as lunch does: the male ambushes the female midflight. Females then lay clusters of white eggs on low plant material, in soil fissures, or in tree bark crevices. I once witnessed a robber fly using her sawlike ovipositor (that's the tube she uses to lay eggs) to insert eggs into the bark of a maple tree at a local playground—something none of the other human mothers there seemed to care about despite my enthusiastic account of what was happening. The eggs hatch and the resulting larvae are also predatory, consuming the eggs, larvae, and adults of soft-bodied insects. Robber fly larvae have a maggotlike appearance but are seldom seen by gardeners. Larvae overwinter in the soil and eventually pupate into adults.

Robber flies are complete carnivores and do not depend directly on plants for nourishment, making no particular flowers or plants more or less attractive to them. They do depend on diverse plantings, however, for habitat—and ample numbers of ill-fated prey.

This female robber fly is dining on a fly while resting on my mailbox. The long, sawlike ovipositor at the tip of her abdomen is used to insert eggs into tree bark or soil fissures.

Syrphid flies look a bit like small bees or wasps, but their single pair of wings easily distinguishes them as flies. After mating in flight as shown here, the female goes on to lay eggs near a colony of soft-bodied insects and each resulting predaceous larva consumes several hundred insects before reaching maturity.

Syrphid flies, hoverflies, flower flies

FAMILY **Syrphidae**

NORTH AMERICAN SPECIES **890+**

Members of this very important group of flies are frequently found hovering around flowers on bright, sunny days. The adults are significant pollinators that consume nectar, pollen, and honeydew. As with all true flies, they have one pair of wings; although at first glance some species may look superficially like small bees or wasps, their wing count is an easy way to separate the two (both bees and wasps have two pairs of wings). Syrphid flies can hover in midflight—hence their other common name of hoverfly. They are often brightly colored with stripes or other markings. Many species mimic bees in their coloration with various patterns of black and yellow, white and black, and occasionally gray or brown. Adults measure 0.16–1 inch (4–25 mm) long, with the majority of species falling somewhere in the middle and only a few at the extremes.

While the adults feed on flower products, their larvae are busy chowing down on various soft-bodied insects, including aphids, thrips, leafhoppers, scales, caterpillars, and others. Members of the subfamily Syrphinae all have predaceous larvae (called maggots—they *are* flies, after all). Larvae of other subfamilies may eat plant tissue, detritus, or even sewage and other waste. The larvae of predatory species are legless maggots 0.04–0.5 inch (1–13 mm)

in length that taper to a point at the head end. They range in color from green to creamy white or brown and wriggle along swinging their heads from side to side until they bump into prey. Each maggot can consume several hundred insects during its three larval instars (life stages between molts) by nabbing the victim with its jaws and sucking it dry. Pupation lasts between one and two weeks or, at season's end, continues through the winter. Many overlapping generations hatch each season.

Adult syrphid fly mouthparts are sponge-like and are used to seep up plant nectar and pollen, both of which must be consumed in ample amounts before reproduction and egg laying can occur. Females of several species are known to determine whether to lay eggs based on how many aphids are present in a colony. The number of eggs she lays is deter-

A pair of newly laid syrphid fly eggs and a hungry syrphid larva are easily found on an aphid-infested leaf—that is, if you know what to look for.

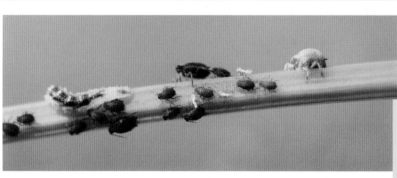

Syrphid larvae find lunch by swinging their heads back and forth until they bump into prey. With so many aphids close by, this one should have no trouble finding something to eat. The brown, swollen aphid on the right has been parasitized by a wasp.

mined by her perception of a pest colony as fit to sustain her young. She can turn her reproductive capabilities on or off depending on semiochemical signals from both the infested plant and the aphids present on it.

Syrphid flies are incapable of stinging or biting and are a welcome sight in the garden. One study found them to be significantly better at locating aphids on collard greens than both ladybugs and green lacewings, though they will not fly on windy, rainy, or cold days. Since adult syrphid flies are completely dependent on pollen and nectar for survival, having plenty of flowering plants around is a must. Several studies have revealed that the number of syrphid fly species present in a field is significantly impacted by the diversity and abundance of flowers located nearby.

With nearly nine hundred different species in North America, syrphid flies are a diverse crew. Adult flies measure anywhere from 0.16 to 1 inch (4–25 mm) and bear assorted markings of black, yellow, white, and brown.

• •

Tachinid flies

FAMILY **Tachinidae**

NORTH AMERICAN SPECIES **1300+**

You may not think a fly to be all that interesting, but I can assure you that this large and diverse family of parasitoids participates in some of the most fascinating interactions in the insect world. Tachinids are among my favorite of all natural enemies, and it surely isn't for their good looks. It is instead for the intriguing lives of these humble-looking creatures.

Tachinid flies are highly variable in their physical appearance. Measuring primarily 0.12–0.55 inch (3–14 mm), with a few larger and smaller species, they most resemble plain old houseflies. Tachinids can be gray, black, or darkly striped and have distinctive hairy bristles protruding from their abdomens. Some species have four black longitudinal stripes on their thorax (the part of the body between the head and the abdomen). The presence of only three stripes indicates it is instead a flesh fly— you know, the ones that eat carrion and poop. A few species of tachinids are bright orange or even metallic blue or green, but most are just plain drab. If you really want to discern them from a housefly, look for a pronounced subscutellum, best described as a distinct rounded ridge on their posterior. I, for one, am not all that interested in examining a fly's posterior, so I rely more on the presence of the abdominal bristles for identification.

Tachinid flies, parasitoids that resemble bristly houseflies, feed on pollen, nectar, and honeydew and are highly variable in appearance and size. Most are dark in color, though a few brightly colored species exist.

Adult tachinids feed on pollen, nectar, and honeydew and are important pollinators. They are very active fliers and are often seen alighting on flowers, fences, rocks, and people. All species of tachinids are parasitoids that use various insects as larval hosts. Most species use caterpillars (cabbage loopers, corn borers, gypsy moths, cutworms, fall armyworms, coddling moth larvae, leaf rollers, bollworms, and many, many others) as hosts while other species parasitize adult and larval beetles, and even various true bugs and sawfly larvae. Tachinids can be generalists that use assorted species as larval hosts or specialists relying on only one species to feed their developing young.

Egg-laying techniques are variable and incredibly intriguing. Some species deposit one or more eggs onto the host insect's exterior or (rarely) inject the egg inside the host. Others lay an egg near a leaf-munching pest; when the egg hatches a few hours later, it is ingested right along with the plant tissue.

Still other species deposit live larvae into the host. For those species that lay eggs on their hosts externally, the 0.04 inch (1 mm) white elongated eggs are easy to spot, particularly when clinging to caterpillars and host insects like Japanese beetles, squash bugs, and stink bugs. Once hatched, the larval maggot begins to consume the host's internal tissues and completes its feeding in four to fourteen days. In most cases, the larva then emerges from the dying host and pupates independently.

Just like other insect predators and parasitoids, tachinids find their host prey based on volatile chemical cues from plants as well as visual and other odor cues. Some species are even lured in by the songs of their hosts, including katydids and crickets.

A female tachinid fly has laid several eggs on this beet armyworm. When the eggs hatch, the resulting larvae burrow into the caterpillar and consume its internal tissues, eventually emerging to pupate and killing the host.

predatory beetles

Beetles are in the order Coleoptera and are characterized by having a pair of hardened, shell-like forewings covering a pair of membranous hind wings. The forewings are held upright during flight. Nearly 400,000 species of beetles have been identified, with several thousand being predatory. Here I detail each of the six main families of predatory beetles and highlight some of the species most commonly encountered in backyard habitats.

• •

Fireflies

FAMILY **Lampyridae**

NORTH AMERICAN SPECIES **approximately 150**

The summer parade of flashing fireflies isn't what it used to be in many parts of North America. These beetles, like many other insects, are suffering from habitat loss and pesticide exposure. In addition, their numbers may be in decline because of light pollution.

Fireflies, also commonly called lightning bugs, use their bioluminescent abdomens to attract mates. The pattern of flashes is unique to each species, as is the color of their glow; flash patterns can be used to distinguish many common species based on the number and duration of their flashes. Males fly around flashing a particular pattern in hopes of finding a female. He signals first, and then she signals her response, often from a low perch. In Great Smoky Mountains National Park,

as well as in certain parts of southeast Asia, synchronous species exist whose flashes can occur simultaneously, with hundreds or even thousands of individuals flashing at precisely the same time. Or they can flash in waves across a landscape. It must be breathtaking.

For those of us living east of the Rocky Mountains, fireflies are a common summer sight. While several species of fireflies are found west of the mountains, they are not luminescent as adults. Fireflies are found on every continent except Antarctica, and while not all species glow as adults, they all do as larvae. Sometimes called glowworms in other parts of the world, larval fireflies emit a steady, dull glow from their abdomens. Adult fireflies eat mostly pollen and nectar, though some species eat nothing at all. The females of one species are known to mimic the flash of another species. When the male arrives in hopes of finding a mate, she attacks and eats him.

Female fireflies lay eggs in the ground (though a few tropical species lay eggs in trees). Favored egg-laying sites include moist places near ponds and streams and in leaf litter. Larval fireflies live under or on the ground and serve as generalist predators, savoring slugs, snails, worms, and other insect larvae. They capture their prey and inject it with a paralytic substance before consuming it. Though they are not frequently seen, predatory larval fireflies have three pairs of legs, are brown to black in color, and have a

Fireflies are found on every continent except Antarctica, though not all species glow as adults. Adult fireflies, like this species of *Photinus*, eat mostly pollen and nectar, though some species don't eat at all.

plated, armorlike appearance. They are finely tapered at the head end with their distinctive glow emanating from their posterior. The intensity and frequency of their glow increases when they are disturbed, likely as a form of protection and a warning signal to would-be predators.

Fireflies overwinter in the soil as larvae. Come spring, the larvae begin to feed and eventually (sometimes several years later) pupate and emerge as adults in summer. The adults have soft bodies and leathery wings with a pronotum (the saddlelike area between the head and the wings) extending over their tiny black head for protection. Both adult and larval fireflies are extremely distasteful, with some species weeping foul-tasting blood from their bodies when threatened.

The bioluminescence of fireflies has been the subject of many studies. Scientists aren't positive how a firefly turns its light on and off, but they do know the glow is caused by the combination of oxygen and a substance called luciferin. The enzyme used in the reaction, called luciferase, along with the luciferin itself, is commonly used in medical research involving cancer, multiple sclerosis, cystic fibrosis, and other medical conditions.

Firefly larvae live under or on the ground and are generalist predators, consuming the likes of slugs, snails, worms, and various insect larvae. Their plated, armorlike exterior affords protection from other predators.

The bioluminescence of fireflies is caused by the combination of oxygen and a substance called luciferin. Because each firefly species emits a unique pattern of flashes meant to attract a mate, flash patterns can be used to identify many common species.

Ground beetles

FAMILY **Carabidae**

NORTH AMERICAN SPECIES **2000+**

Unless you garden at night, you're not likely to encounter ground beetles on a regular basis even though they are very common. These nocturnal predators are found under logs and rocks during the day but come out at night to scour the soil surface for prey. They are highly variable in size and habit, but both adults and larvae hunt at ground level and commonly consume mites, snails, earthworms, slugs, caterpillars, and lots of other insects. Ground beetles can eat more than their own body weight in prey insects each and every day. Once a victim has been captured, the beetle regurgitates digestive fluids to soften its meal before consumption. Most species are shiny and black and have rigid, grooved wing covers.

Larval ground beetles in the family Carabidae use their large curved jaws to capture prey on the soil surface. I found this one under a stepping-stone in my garden.

Ladybugs, lady beetles, ladybirds

FAMILY **Coccinellidae**

NORTH AMERICAN SPECIES **480+**

In the world of beneficial insects, ladybugs have become the red-and-black-polka-dotted poster children. Unless you've been hiding under a rock, you know how good ladybugs are for the garden, and you may think you already know everything there is to know about them. But you'd be wrong. First off, there's a ton of physical diversity in the ladybug family; not everyone wears the same red-and-black uniform. A significant number of species have completely different coloration. Ladybugs can be brown, yellow, cream, orange, black, gray, or pink. They can have lots of spots, spots that meld together, or no spots at all. They can be striped, banded, or mottled. They can even have blue eyes. Because of all the physical diversity in this clan, learning to recognize some common familial traits may be a better way of identifying this important insect family than just seeing red.

Ladybugs aren't true bugs at all but members of the beetle order. In many parts of the world they are known as lady beetles, which is, in fact, a far more appropriate name for them. Species range in size from minute (0.04 inch or 1 mm) to moderate (0.4 inch or 10 mm) and everything in between. All are dome shaped with hard wing covers called elytra, very short antennae, six legs, and an enlarged pronotum,

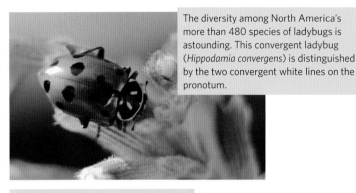

The diversity among North America's more than 480 species of ladybugs is astounding. This convergent ladybug (*Hippodamia convergens*) is distinguished by the two convergent white lines on the pronotum.

Anatis labiculata, the fifteen-spotted ladybug, is gray as a young adult but ages to this beautiful burgundy.

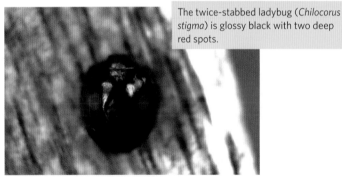

The twice-stabbed ladybug (*Chilocorus stigma*) is glossy black with two deep red spots.

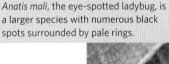

Anatis mali, the eye-spotted ladybug, is a larger species with numerous black spots surrounded by pale rings.

under which the head can retreat for protection. The number of spots, as well as their locations and shapes, is genetically predetermined and has nothing to do with the insect's age, despite what folklore may tell us. All ladybugs are completely devoid of spots when they first emerge from pupation as adults.

Nearly all ladybug species are predaceous as both adults and larvae (only two family members, the Mexican bean beetle and the squash beetle, are herbivorous). Many of North America's ladybug species are generalist predators consuming insect prey such as aphids, scale, mites, mealybugs, small caterpillars, insect eggs and pupae, whiteflies, mites, psyllids, and each other. A small handful of species even feed on mildew. Within the ladybug family are also a plethora of specialists known to consume only one type of adelgid or mealybug or mite. All predaceous adult ladybugs also need pollen and nectar to survive and reproduce. Idiosyncratic names like eye-spotted lady beetle, three-banded lady beetle, ash gray lady beetle, seven-spotted lady beetle, twice-stabbed lady beetle, multicolored Asian lady beetle, and many others identify some of the physical features of these species.

Ladybug eggs are elongated ovals, and the larvae are small six-legged, flattened, alligator-like creatures that are darkly colored with assorted markings, though a few species are brown or covered with white waxy hairs. The larvae pass through four instars over the course of about two weeks, during which time they are completely carnivorous, eating only their insect prey. They then pupate in a shell and emerge as an adult a week or two later.

Most species overwinter as adults, hiding in tree bark, natural crevices, and structures. The introduced multicolored Asian lady beetle is known for its nuisance habit of overwintering in homes. After migrating, the native convergent lady beetle can be found hibernating by the thousands on mountaintops in some parts of the American West (these insects are often "harvested" for sale in garden centers and nurseries). Some ladybugs can bite, and many can secrete a smelly substance from their joints when disturbed.

The multicolored Asian lady beetle, along with several other introduced species, is known to outcompete many native species in intraguild predation. One study that paired native ladybugs with introduced species both with and without alternate prey determined that in both cases the native beetles were far more likely to be the victims than the perpetrators of intraguild predation. The introduced species always consumed the native. Native ladybugs face many challenges resulting from the increased rate of intraguild predation by introduced species. Some researchers believe this is likely contributing to the population decline noted in many native ladybug species. They also frequently fall victim to lots of other generalist predators as well as several parasitoids.

Ladybug eggs are yellow and bullet shaped.

An introduced species, the checker spot ladybug (*Propylea quatuordecimpunctata*) is yellow with a black checkerboard pattern.

Ladybug larvae are nearly as diverse as the adults. They are small and alligator-like in appearance, with assorted markings and coloration. All are predaceous, feeding on various insect prey.

finding the lost ladybugs

Based on an interview with Leslie Allee, PhD, director of outreach and education for the Lost Ladybug Project, Cornell University, Ithaca, New York

THE NINE-SPOTTED LADYBUG is New York's state insect, but for more than twenty years no one had actually seen any of them there. What was once the most common ladybug species in the northeastern United States had seemingly vanished. Two other native ladybug species that were once very common across eastern North America, the two-spotted and the transverse, were also becoming scarce there although they were still found in the West and Midwest. At the same time, the populations of two introduced species, the multicolored Asian ladybug and the seven-spotted ladybug, were taking off. "The timing of these population shifts was suspicious and we wanted to know why it was happening," explains Leslie Allee.

The Lost Ladybug Project was founded in 2000 by John Losey, an entomology professor at Cornell University, in hopes of using citizen science to help track the numbers and locations of different ladybug species in the state of New York. Master Gardener, school, and community groups began to take part in ladybug population surveys in 2004 by searching for and photo-graphing every ladybug they could find. Allee joined the project in 2005 to help with its development. After gaining support from the National Science Foundation, the project went online and national in 2008. As of 2012, the Lost Ladybug Project had collected more than 19,000 ladybug images from every state in the United States, and from Canada and parts of Mexico. "It's not an exact science, but it gives us a good idea of what species live where," says Allee.

In 2006, during the development of the national survey, a pair of kids found a nine-spotted ladybug in Virginia—proof that the species still existed in the East. Then in the summer of 2011, a group of people participating in a ladybug search sponsored by a local land trust struck gold: they found the first nine-spotted ladybug in New York State in more than twenty years. It was discovered on an organic farm, and the researchers who returned to the farm later that season found a whole colony of nine-spotteds. They were unable, though, to find any others in searching several surrounding farms.

The Lost Ladybug Project has also done laboratory research to help determine why native species are in decline. The tests confirm that native species are being outcompeted by introduced species, partly because the introduced species are quicker to reproduce and because they eat more. Reproductive interactions between the native and introduced species may also be playing a role, although it's not clear how.

The researchers thought that perhaps the nine-spotted was breeding with the seven-spotted and all the resulting offspring had only seven spots, but they have found that it's not that simple.

In addition to the 2006 and 2011 discoveries of nine-spotted ladybugs, project participants have also established that the two-spotted ladybug is not gone from the East, despite the dramatic drop in its numbers. These ladybugs have been identified in New York, New England, and up into Canada. And the existence of a transverse ladybug has been reported in northern Michigan, the farthest east they've been found so far.

Thanks to the help of interested citizens, the Lost Ladybug Project has the largest and most geographically widespread ladybug database in existence, and with it they have confirmed the recent shift in ladybug populations across North America. They have discovered that slightly more than half of the ladybugs found in North America are foreign species, with the multicolored Asian ladybug being the dominant species.

To continue tracking ladybugs across North America, the Lost Ladybug Project needs help. "We want to expand the number of scouting groups going out," explains Allee. "We need 4-H groups, garden clubs, public libraries, schools, and other organizations to organize searches and submit their photographs to us." Allee encourages groups and individuals to take pictures of each and every ladybug they find,

regardless of the species, regardless of whether it's native or introduced, and even regardless of whether they're sure it's a ladybug. "We want pictures of them all, not just the rare ones." To learn more about the Lost Ladybug Project and submit pictures of your own discoveries, go to www.lostladybug.org.

Introduced multicolored Asian ladybugs are known to outcompete many native ladybug species. They are large and very round, and have a huge range of coloration and spot patterns.

Rove beetles are distinguished by their short wing covers and exposed, segmented abdomen. Adult beetles like the one shown here consume the same prey as their fast-moving larvae—termites, slugs, snails, root maggots, and various other insects.

Rove beetles

FAMILY Staphylinidae

NORTH AMERICAN SPECIES 3000+

This family has the honor of being one of the largest families of beetles in North America. A distinctive feature of most rove beetles is the short wing covers that leave their segmented abdomens exposed. When threatened, many species of rove beetles curl their abdomens upward in scorpion fashion. No need to worry, though, as these beetles have no stinger. They are generally brown to black and measure 0.08–0.78 inch (2–20 mm) in length (though some species can reach much larger).

Rove beetles are predators of insects that feed on decaying organic matter (a handful of parasitic species exist as well). They commonly consume bark beetles, slugs, snails, ants, termites, root maggots, and many others and are found in plant debris, in manure and compost piles, under stones, and in woodlands. Their fast-moving larvae feed on the same prey species by capturing them with sickle-shaped jaws. A few species can produce skin-blistering chemicals or defensive odors when attacked.

Soldier beetles, leatherwings

FAMILY Cantharidae

NORTH AMERICAN SPECIES 470

As adults, all species of solider beetles have soft, leathery wings; they fly well and serve to pollinate various flowering plants. Larval soldier beetles live in leaf litter and under rocks, logs, and debris. Larvae feed primarily at night and are fast movers with large, grasping jaws that capture insect eggs and prey insects, including grasshopper eggs, caterpillars, aphids, and mealybugs. Adults consume nectar, with many species also eating aphids and other insects. Both adult and larval soldier beetles can exude foul defensive chemicals to aid in protecting them from other predators. In the eastern United States, the orange and black Pennsylvania leatherwing is a common sight, while the brown leatherwing is more common in the West.

Soldier beetles, like this adult Pennsylvania leatherwing (*Chauliognathus pensylvanicus*), serve as pollinators as well as predators. Larval soldier beetles are primarily nocturnal feeders that consume various insects and insect eggs.

The six-spotted tiger beetle (*Cicindela sexguttata*) uses its long, thin legs to stalk insect prey.

Tiger beetles use curved mandibles to capture and consume their prey.

Tiger beetles

FAMILY **Cicindelidae**

NORTH AMERICAN SPECIES **100+**

The most beautiful of the predatory beetles, tiger beetles come in an array of colors and patterns. While black is certainly a common color, so are brilliant purple, deep red, iridescent green, shining blue, and bright yellow. Some species are spotted or patterned while others are solid colored. All tiger beetles have long, thin legs (perfect for running in short, fast bursts), an elongated body, and a head with pronounced eyes. On most species, the head is wider than the body. Body lengths range from 0.27 to 2.75 inches (7–70 mm), with only a few species falling at the extremes.

Adult tiger beetles capture their prey with long, curved mandibles and then use digestive enzymes to partially digest the victim before it is mashed by the mandibles and consumed. Unlike other predatory beetles, larval tiger beetles reside in open cylindrical burrows in the ground. These slender white grubs position themselves in the burrow with their head blocking the opening. When an unfortunate prey insect happens by, the larva extends its body and reaches out in a back flip to nab lunch. The prey insect is then dragged into the burrow and quickly consumed.

parasitic wasps

Parasitic wasps are a very complex group of parasitoids with a tremendous amount of diversity in both their individual appearance and life cycle. To speak of them without generalizing to some extent is nearly impossible. But just because I'm simplifying the details of these insects, do not value them any less. Parasitic wasps are highly sophisticated and intriguing insects—and they are my favorites of all the natural enemies I highlight in this book. I feel certain that most gardeners don't really need or want to know exactly how each and every species lives and procreates; if you do, you are probably already an entomologist. So instead I will give you the basics of the role these creatures play in controlling pests and the details of a few easy-to-identify and highly visible families so that you can discover their activities in your own backyard.

In the insect order Hymenoptera, which includes the bees, wasps, ants, and sawflies, is a suborder called Apocrita. Here are categorized the bees, ants, and wasps. Since this category of animals is so very large, it is commonly divided into two artificial groupings: Aculeta (which includes the bees, ants, and nonparasitic wasps) and Parasitica (which includes the more than forty families of parasitic wasps). The Parasitica group contains the species I am highlighting in this section, but you should be aware that the Aculeta group also consists of largely beneficial species: bees pollinate, ants

break down organic matter, and nonparasitic wasps like the paper wasp, hornet, hunting wasp, and yellow jacket feed their young both living and dead insect prey. They too play a valuable role in our yards and gardens. The Parasitica group, however, contains those families that often leave my jaw dropped in awe when I spot them at work in my garden.

Parasitic wasps can be smaller than a gnat or as long as your pinky finger. Nearly all of them use other insects as hosts for their young, with many using only one or two species of insects for this task. Most often the females lay eggs singly or in groups on, or inside of, the host. The larvae then hatch and develop inside of the host, consuming the nonvital tissues first to ensure the host survives

Though nonparasitic wasps like this yellow jacket (*Vespula* species) are capable of stinging, they are terrific predators, feeding their young with insect prey. This one is tearing apart a pest caterpillar.

A *Cotesia* wasp has parasitized this hornworm and the fully developed larvae have begun to emerge from the hornworm's body to spin their silken cocoons. In a little less than a week, the adult wasps will emerge from the cocoons and fly off.

This female wasp is inserting a single egg into an aphid.

until the larvae are ready to pupate into adults. Though you will probably never encounter the larvae themselves, they are often cream-colored, legless, maggotlike creatures. Parasitic wasps attack almost every group of insects, including aphids, beetles, flies, scales, true bugs, and caterpillars of every sort.

Most species are not capable of stinging people, and what may look like a nasty stinger protruding from the abdomen of the females of some species is actually an ovipositor. Different parasitic wasps have different egg-laying equipment. Depending on what is being parasitized, the ovipositor can be short and spiky, long and wispy, or somewhere in between. Species that penetrate wood to parasitize the larval insects inside have different equipment from the ones that merely puncture the skin of an aphid. Such body structures in this group have certainly evolved with an incredible exactitude.

Here are a handful of commonly encountered parasitic wasp families to look for in your garden.

Braconid wasps

FAMILY **Braconidae**

NORTH AMERICAN SPECIES **1700+**

Members of this family average less than 0.5 inch (13 mm) long. Within this family are many species in the genus *Cotesia*. These parasitoids attack caterpillars, and gardeners can often find their ricelike white cocoons clinging to tomato and tobacco hornworms in the summer. Different *Cotesia* species also parasitize cabbage worms, cutworms, corn earworms, gypsy moths, tobacco budworms, and other caterpillars. *Cotesia* species mature from egg to adult in fifteen to thirty days, spending only two of those days as eggs and the remainder as larvae. Once the larvae have matured inside their host, they chew small holes through the skin and spin external cocoons in which they pupate for four to six days. Once mature, the adult wasps pop the top off the cocoon and fly off.

Also within the family Braconidae is the

Each of the aphid mummies in this colony contains a wasp larva.

A few days later, an adult wasp emerges from the parasitized aphid via a circular hole chewed in the mummy's back.

subfamily Aphidiinae. This group uses only aphids as larval hosts. There are approximately 114 different Aphidiinae species in North America, with most of them measuring a mere 0.1 inch (2.5 mm)—certainly small enough to maneuver their way around a colony of tiny aphids. They are incredibly common, and spotting evidence of these wasps is as easy as reaching for your hand lens. Aphidiinae attack their hosts by laying a single egg in each aphid. The larva hatches soon after and excavates the aphid, creating a swollen brown so-called aphid mummy. Once the larva has matured, the adult wasp chews a circular hole in the mummy's back, crawls out, and flies off.

Chalcid wasps

SUPERFAMILY **Chalcidoidea**

NORTH AMERICAN SPECIES **thousands**

Chalcid wasps parasitize everything from caterpillars and flies to beetles and true bugs (and a few even feed on plant tissue). With about twenty families in this group and thousands of species, they are incredibly useful to gardeners. Measuring 0.02–0.31 inch (0.4–8 mm), these minute wasps are often dark in color but are sometimes metallic.

Within the superfamily Chalcidoidea are members of the genus *Trichogramma*. These species are specialist parasites that target only insect eggs. They are often sold by insectaries to help control common agricultural pests and are among the smallest insects on the planet, often measuring less than 0.04 inch (1 mm) in length.

The empty larval skins of clubtail dragonflies (family Gomphidae) cling to a log. Dragonflies and damselflies spend the majority of their lives underwater as larvae known as naiads; most species live only a month as adults.

Ichneumon wasps

FAMILY **Ichneumonidae**

NORTH AMERICAN SPECIES **3300**

While many species of ichneumon wasps are extremely tiny, others are very large (up to 1.5 inches or 40 mm!). All are slender with long antennae. Many females have a highly noticeable ovipositor; it is sometimes longer than the insect's body. Ichneumon wasps can be yellow to black or have patterns of various colors. They use caterpillars, the wood-boring grubs of various beetles, and other insects as hosts.

dragonflies and damselflies

The order Odonata encompasses two suborders, Epiprocta (dragonflies) and Zygoptera (damselflies). With more than 425 different species in North America, these insects are distinguished as having two pairs of functional membranous wings (unlike the true flies, which only have one). They have large eyes and elongated bodies.

Dragonflies are among the fastest fliers in the insect world. They are swift and agile aviators and can turn on a dime. Damselflies?

Well, not so much. Though these cousins have much in common, their flight operations are slightly different; damselflies flutter about a bit more casually. Despite their differences, both damsels and dragons are stealth predators, as both adults and nymphs. As generalist predators, the adults feed on mosquitoes, flies, bees, ants, moths, wasps, and pretty much anything else they can nab midflight. They then find a perch and consume their victim using the teeth in their lower jaw.

Both dragonflies and damselflies have two pairs of translucent wings that move independently of each other and can be used

Dragonflies like this window skimmer (*Libellula luctuosa*) rest with their wings open, while damselflies fold their wings together. Both are predators that feed on various insects, including mosquitoes, moths, and flies.

to steer the insect like rudders. A quick and easy way to distinguish the two groups is to observe the way the wings are held when the insect is resting. Dragonflies lack a hinge to close their wings, so they rest with their wings out flat. They also have two large compound eyes that face forward and sometimes touch. Damselflies fold their wings together up over their long delicate abdomen when they are perched, much like a resting butterfly. The compound eyes of damselflies are wide set. Both dragonflies and damselflies also have three simple eyes grouped together between their stubby antennae.

Dragonflies and damselflies are most often found near water as they spend their larval stage on the bottom of ponds, streams, lakes, creeks, and rivers. The naiads (the technical name for their larvae) breathe through gills and eat the likes of tadpoles, snails, mosquito larvae, and other aquatic insects. The naiad stage lasts anywhere from eleven months to several years, depending on the species, while the adult stage lasts a mere month. Naiads undergo a series of molts as they grow. Just before the final molt the insect crawls from the water and positions itself on a rock or plant stem, head pointed upward.

This pair of American bluets (*Enallagma* species) are in a mating wheel. These damselflies hold this heart-shaped pose for fifteen minutes or more until copulation is complete.

The larval skin then splits and the partially emerged adult hangs upside down until its skin hardens. Eventually the wings fill with blood and the insect is able to fly. The whole process takes less than an hour. They soon develop their full coloration and are ready to begin the mating process a week or two later.

Each female may mate and lay eggs several times. If you've ever spotted a pair of these insects flying in tandem with each other (usually with the tip of the male's abdomen attached to the female just behind her head), you've seen the beginning stage of the mating process. When the female is ready, she raises her abdomen forward to meet the underside of the male's abdomen just behind his wings. Here is where he stores his sperm (it's produced farther down his abdomen, but he transfers it here before the mating process begins). The pair remain in this heart-shaped pose, known as a mating wheel, for fifteen minutes or more, often flying about in the process.

Some species lay eggs by flying over the water's surface and repeatedly dabbing their abdomen into the water, each time depositing an egg. Other species insert eggs into plant tissue or glue them to rocks or plants in shallow water. The resulting naiads have a harpoonlike jaw that rapidly juts out from their mouth, nabs prey, and then conveniently deposits it back into their mouth.

Common North American dragonfly species include the green darner, a green-and-blue beauty 3 inches (76 mm) long that amazingly migrates from the northern United States to Mexico every year; the common whitetail, with males that are white with broad black bands on the wings and females that are brown with black wing splotches; the roseate skimmer, with rose pink males and orange females; the four-spotted skimmer, with brown abdomens and four small spots on the wings; and the comet darner, a large species with males having a green thorax and red abdomen and females being brown with blue dots.

lacewings

To say the lacewings are a complicated bunch would be an understatement. Simplifying them seems to undervalue their presence in the landscape, but without some generalizations, a gardener can quickly get buried in lacewing particulars. Lacewings are in the order Neuroptera, and there are thousands of North American species. All undergo complete metamorphosis, passing through four life stages—egg, larva, pupa, and adult. Adults hold their wings in a folded rooftop over their bodies, and nymphs have sickle-shaped jaws for grabbing and consuming prey. Of approximately fifteen North American families, the three described here contain the most widespread species of lacewings.

Members of the family Coniopterygidae are often called dustywings and are a mere 0.125 inch (3 mm) long. They are predators of aphids, scale insects, mites, and other very small insects. They get their name from the dusty-white powdery wax covering the adult's body. Dustywings are often found on conifers and other trees but are seldom seen by gardeners.

Lacewings in the other two families, Hemerobiidae (brown lacewings) and Chrysopidae (green lacewings), are far more ordinary in the garden and frequently cling to illuminated window screens at night. Both brown and green lacewings have large net-like wings with complex veining. They have narrow bodies with slender legs and arching antennae. Adults of most species are nocturnal. But here is where the similarities between the two families stop.

The green lacewing family comprises more than twelve hundred species, and in order to tell them apart you need to carefully examine their genitalia—a task I will gratefully leave to the lacewing experts of the world. Most green lacewing eggs are laid individually or in groups on half-inch-high stalks, lending the appearance of little lollipops in a row. The hatching larvae are born voracious. As generalist predators, they use their large mandibles to capture a wide range of prey, including small caterpillars, aphids, mealybugs, beetles, lace bugs, whiteflies, assorted insect larvae,

Dustywings are among the most prominent lacewing families, though they are seldom seen by gardeners. Most dustywings spend their time on conifers and other trees, feeding on numerous kinds of small insects.

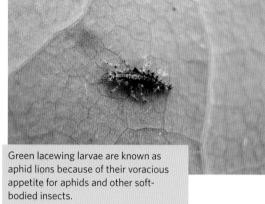

Green lacewing larvae are known as aphid lions because of their voracious appetite for aphids and other soft-bodied insects.

Both adult and larval brown lacewings are predaceous, with many species being specialist predators. This larva is seen with its aphid prey.

Green lacewings lay their eggs on small stalks.

and, if necessary, each other. These larvae are often called aphid lions because of their tendency to snack on aphids.

Immature green lacewings look like tiny brown alligators with a large pair of curved jaws for puncturing prey. Some species are known to cover their bodies with debris for camouflage. Larvae pupate attached to plant material or structures while encased in a round silken cocoon; many species overwinter

Adult brown lacewings are smaller than their green cousins.

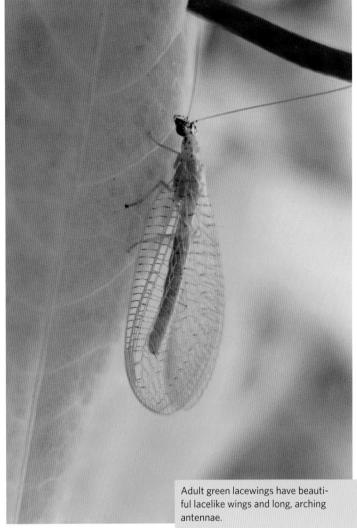
Adult green lacewings have beautiful lacelike wings and long, arching antennae.

as pupae. Adult green lacewings of many species feed on pollen, nectar, and honeydew, though adults in the genus *Chrysopa* are predaceous. They can range in color from brilliant emerald green to soft yellow-green, with wings measuring 0.4–0.8 inch (10–20 mm) long.

Some species of green lacewings sing to attract a mate, though their songs are of such low frequency that they are nearly inaudible to humans unless your ear is right up against the insect. These songs are produced through rapid motions of the insect's abdomen that cause the plant material on which they are perched to vibrate. Males and females of the same species exchange nearly identical songs during courtship, with each song's pattern being particular to the given species. If you are interested in hearing the beautifully haunting, rhythmic songs of these lacewings, you may be able to have a listen online by searching for "lacewing songs."

Brown lacewings are often smaller than green lacewing species and have a wing length of 0.12–0.7 inch (3–18 mm). They are predators in both adult and larval stages.

Many species are specialist predators feeding on a particular type of aphid or mealybug. Most are drab brown, though a few green and yellow species occur. Unlike their green cousins, brown lacewings lay their eggs without stalks, though they too hatch into free-roaming, predaceous larvae.

A two-week-old Chinese mantid hangs out on a yarrow blossom. This introduced species is one of about twenty different mantid species found in North America.

praying mantids

Mantids are among the most fascinating of nature's creatures. They are in the family Mantidae within the order Orthoptera (which also includes grasshoppers, katydids, walking sticks, and the like). The name *praying mantis* is commonly heard in reference to members of this insect group, but *praying mantid* is actually the appropriate name. This is because only some members of this group of insects are in the genus *Mantis*, while others are in a number of other genera. The name *mantid* refers to the entire group and thus is the correct name.

Most gardeners are surprised to find out there are some twenty different species of praying mantids in North America. Three are introduced and the rest are natives. The most commonly encountered mantids in most of the United States, however, are introduced species. All mantid species have an elongated thorax, lending the appearance of a long neck.

Atop the thorax is the insect's head; a mantid, unlike other insects, can swivel its head a full 180 degrees in both directions. Mantids have a large compound eye on each side of their squat, triangular head and three small, simple eyes situated in a triangle between the antennae. Immature praying mantids look much like adults but are smaller and lack wings. Most species hang from a branch to molt five to ten times before fully maturing.

Mantids are patient ambush predators able to wait long periods of time for prey to happen by. They are generalist predators who are quite fond of eating nearly any insect they can nab, including moths, crickets, grasshoppers, flies, beetles, bees, and caterpillars. Larger species have even been known to capture and consume frogs, lizards, and small birds. Though it was once thought that mantids are exclusively predators, a few recent

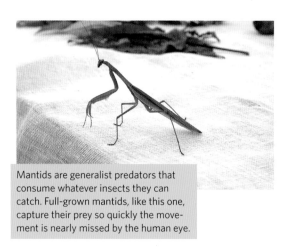

Mantids are generalist predators that consume whatever insects they can catch. Full-grown mantids, like this one, capture their prey so quickly the movement is nearly missed by the human eye.

Praying mantid egg cases appear as a spongelike mass clinging to twigs and stems. The globular shape of this egg cluster indicates it is from an introduced Chinese mantid; the egg sac of another common species, the European mantid, is more elongated.

studies have noted that certain species also eat pollen, both as youngsters and adults. Mantids spend less than 5 percent of their time eating and the rest waiting to snatch their quarry with their large raptorial forelegs. These legs are studded with spikes to secure their prey as they consume it in mammalian fashion with grinding bites. Mantids strike their prey so quickly that the movement is nearly missed by the human eye.

Females are distinguished from males by their larger, heavier abdomens. Mating takes place in autumn, with some species participating in an elaborate courtship display of dancing, flexing, and posing. The supposed sexual cannibalism of the females of certain species is overdramatized; the ladies consume their mates only about a quarter of the time when the insects are reared in captivity and less frequently in the wild, though when it does occur, it's a sight to behold. If the cannibalism occurs pre-mating, the male continues to copulate despite his lack of a head, or if the cannibalism happens post-breeding, the female simply captures and consumes him whole or in part. I guess the lesson is to be thankful you aren't a praying mantid.

Most species produce only one generation per year, with eggs being laid in masses encased in a protective layer of dry foam secured to twigs, stems, or structures each autumn. Come spring, the eggs hatch and the tiny nymphs begin to stalk their prey imme-

diately. If no prey are available, mantids will readily turn to cannibalism at all life stages. When threatened, mantids may stand up with their forelegs raised and wings spread out—an imposing posture they are able to hold for a surprising amount of time.

The most common introduced species is the European mantid. It has both brown and green forms, with green being the more common of the two. European mantids have a circular bull's-eye mark on the inside of their forelegs, measure 3 inches (76 mm) in length, and lay eggs in an elongated ootheca (egg sac). Chinese mantids are also common in much of North America, and their egg cases are often sold for release into gardens. Chinese mantids are 3–5 inches (76–127 mm) long and are generally brown with green and yellow striping on the sides of the wings. Their ootheca is more globular. The third introduced species, the narrow-winged mantid, is found in the southern United States.

Native mantid species include the California mantid, common in the West, and the Carolina mantid, a native of the Southeast. These two species are distinguished by their 2-inch (51-mm) length and shorter wing covers that don't extend all the way to the ends of their abdomens. The ground mantid, at 1.5 inches (38 mm) long, is flightless and indigenous to the western prairies. Other North American native mantids include southern species like the grizzled mantid (which resembles lichens or tree bark), the American grass mantid (which looks much like—yep, you guessed it—a blade of grass), the Arizona and Texas unicorn mantids (which are super cool looking with a knobby "horn" projecting from the front of their heads), and a dozen or so other regional species.

arachnids

Members of the class Arachnida aren't insects at all. They are distinguished from insects by their eight legs and a body with two distinct segments rather than three. They also lack antennae. Among the arachnids are two groups of arthropods that play a critical role in controlling garden pests, and while neither of them probably top your love list, at the very least they should be valued for their role in pest management.

● ●

Predatory mites

FAMILY Phytoseiidae, Anystidae, Laelapidae, Stigmaeidae, and others

NORTH AMERICAN SPECIES thousands

Though multiple families of mites contain predatory species, the most important family of predatory mites is Phytoseiidae (its members are called phytoseiid mites). Mites are not

Tiny predatory mites in the family Phytoseiidae are important predators of many different pest species. The predatory mite shown here (*Amblyseius cucumeris*) feeds on thrips, two-spotted spider mites, and a few other mite species.

insects but rather members of the arachnid class. They do not have the antennae, wings, and segmented bodies of insects. Adult mites have eight legs and are very small, generally 0.004–0.031 inch (0.1–0.8 mm) in length. Mites are often thought of as plant pests and indeed many of them are, including the seemingly ever-present two-spotted spider mite. However, scores of predatory mite species feed on pest mites and many different insects.

Phytoseiid mites are often categorized based on their preferred prey. Type I mites are specialist predators that feed on only one type of pest mite (the two-spotted spider mite, for example). They are very efficient predators and can significantly reduce pest mite numbers quickly. However, once the prey population declines, they often do too. Type II mite species are not as specialized as Type I and feed on other mite prey if their preferred species isn't available. Their populations are far more self-sustaining as long as alternative prey species are available. Type III mites are generalist predators that eat various mite species as well as other pest insects like thrips, whitefly nymphs, scale crawlers, leafhoppers, fungus gnats, and psyllids. Type III predatory mites are also able to survive on pollen and plant fluids when prey are absent. These species are a constant in most gardens since they can survive on such a varied diet, though they are less effective at gaining rapid control over pest numbers.

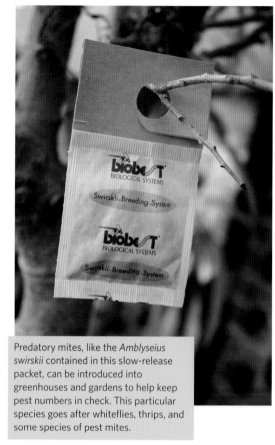

Predatory mites, like the *Amblyseius swirskii* contained in this slow-release packet, can be introduced into greenhouses and gardens to help keep pest numbers in check. This particular species goes after whiteflies, thrips, and some species of pest mites.

No matter which species of predatory mites are present in your garden (and there are likely to be many), it's always difficult to distinguish them from pest species. Predaceous mites are pear shaped and shiny and have longer legs and slightly larger bodies than their plant-eating cousins. They can be translucent to reddish orange, depending on the color of their most recent meal. Having a 10× hand lens or magnifying glass around is the only way to gain an appreciation for the actions of these tiny predators. A relatively simple way to distinguish predatory mites from their prey is to watch a mite colony carefully. Predaceous species move around actively searching for prey, while plant-feeding mites tend to stay put. Blowing on a leaf housing a population of mites often causes the predatory species to scamper while those feeding on plant tissue remain stationary. The eggs of predatory mites are also distinctive. They are larger and more elliptical (egg shaped) than the rounded eggs of their pesty cousins.

Predatory mites are quite good at maintaining populations of pest mites and other prey insects at manageable levels. They produce multiple generations per year thanks to their rapid reproduction rate and short life span. Depending on temperature and humidity levels, predatory mite species can complete their life cycle in as few as three weeks. Female phytoseiid mites lay between forty and sixty eggs in their lifetime. Eggs hatch within a day or two of being laid. The resulting six-legged nymphs pass through two stages in as little as one to three days, with adults living about twenty days. During its development, each predatory mite can consume up to twenty pest mites per day.

Predatory mites feed with a pair of needlelike chelicerae (the same mouthpart as all arachnids, including spiders and ticks). They use them to pierce their prey and suck out the internal juices; pest mites use them to pierce plant tissue and drink the plant's fluids. Predatory mites are extremely prone to the effects of miticides and chemical insecticides. The use of such chemicals often causes a rapid rebound in pest mite numbers as a result of the elimination of predatory species. Avoid using these products. If pest mites are an issue in the orchard, a single application of horticultural oil when trees are dormant will kill the exposed eggs of pest mites. Since predatory mites overwinter as adults in sheltered sites, they are often unaffected by the spray.

● ●

Spiders

ORDER **Araneae**

NORTH AMERICAN SPECIES **3000+**

Spiders are included in the list of good bugs because they are extremely valuable predators that consume thousands of different prey species. All spiders have two body parts, eight legs, four pairs of eyes, and no antennae. The last two abdominal segments are modified into one to four pairs of spinnerets, which secrete silken threads. All spiders produce silk, even those that do not spin webs. All spiders also have chelicerae, mouthparts that include fangs, and most, but not all, have venom. The large majority of spiders, however, do not inflict painful or harmful bites, nor are any of

Cursorial spiders, like this jumping spider (family Salticidae) chowing on a bagworm, hunt by stalking and capturing their prey rather than trapping it in a web. Being highly mobile and consuming a broad range of pest insects, they play a very important role in the garden.

them out to get you. Ignore them and they'll ignore you (a personal mantra of mine based on my dislike of having spiders anywhere near my body).

Spiders are very valuable to the farm and garden. They prey on insects and other spiders by trapping them in a web or pouncing on them. The former are known as web builders and the latter as cursorial spiders (also sometimes called wandering or hunting spiders). Prey are consumed in both groups after liquefaction with digestive enzymes. After breeding, females spin silken egg cases, each housing hundreds of eggs, and position them on webs or attach them to their abdomens. Some species die immediately after egg laying while many others care for the young spiderlings by protecting them on the web or toting them around on their backs.

Web-spinning spiders detect their prey through vibration and visual signals. Cursorial spiders use the same cues to spot and stalk potential prey. Cursorial spiders are of particular importance to gardeners and farmers as they are highly mobile and can travel to find prey, though some groups—the crab spiders, for example—spend nearly all their lives waiting in a single flower for unfortunate pollinators to come by so they can nab them and have them for dinner.

Numerous studies have proven again and again that spiders consume many herbivorous agricultural pests, including insect eggs, beetles, aphids, cutworms, fire ants, fourlined plant bugs, spider mites, squash bugs, budworms, caterpillars, and asparagus beetles. One study found that hunting spiders in some crops do at least a quarter of the total predation, much of it taking place at night.

It's also been revealed that many cursorial spiders aren't exclusively carnivorous. They also feed on nectar, and those that do so on a regular basis grow faster, survive longer, and reproduce more. They can detect the odor of nectar and can even learn to follow cues to obtain it. Fields offering large quantities of nectar have higher populations of spiders and often greater overall predation.

Web-spinning spiders, like this visually striking orchard orbweaver (*Leucauge venusta*), detect their prey through a combination of visual and vibrational cues. Though not all spiders spin webs, all have the ability to produce silk.

gardening for bugs

where plants and insects intersect

I magine that the only way you could eat was by licking. Or that you had a straw instead of a mouth. Or, heaven forbid, that you had to vomit on your food before you could chow down. Such is the consumptive life of many an insect. Humans, of course, have a mouth that opens with a hinged jaw and teeth that bite and grind. Insects, too, have evolved specialized mouthparts perfectly suited for their own personal style of ingestion. While there are certainly insects with mouthparts similar to ours (have you ever watched a praying mantid crunch down a grasshopper with its sideways-moving jaw?), the ways insects eat are nearly as diverse as the insects themselves.

This is important information because understanding the feeding requirements of

Beneficial insects rely on plants for food, shelter, and egg-laying sites, but not just any plant will do. Each species of insect has evolved to rely on a particular flower shape and size for nectar and pollen. Insectary gardens that include a multitude of different plants and floral architectures support the broadest diversity of insects.

beneficial insects can help you think about what to plant in your insect-friendly habitat. You see, not all flowers are appropriate food sources for every beneficial. In essence, good bugs need to find flowers that match their mouths. Nectar-feeding beneficials seek out a particular floral architecture in order to readily access nectar. In the fact, the diets of many beneficials are a complex combination of nectar, pollen, and prey that differs greatly depending on the species. Precisely which plants we decide to put in our yards can influence the health and happiness of our resident good bugs. This chapter gives you the background about bug feeding to help you understand why plant choice is so important.

of insect mouthparts and meals

Consider the rostrum—the long swordlike mouthpart possessed by all true bugs in the suborder Heteroptera. Herbivorous true bugs use their rostrum to pierce and suck the juices from plant tissue. Predaceous true bugs, like damsel and assassin bugs, use the rostrum to stab and suck the juices from prey. Insects with chewing mouthparts like beetles and grasshoppers, on the other hand, feed not by sucking the juices from plants or prey but rather by grinding them up with their jaws. And adult butterflies and moths drink nectar through a strawlike mouthpart called a

Insects have evolved mouthparts perfectly suited to their consumptive habits. This fritillary butterfly uses its strawlike proboscis to drink nectar from flowers.

proboscis, while as immature caterpillars they chomp leaves or other plant tissue. As you can see from just these few examples, mouthpart morphology plays a huge role in how and what insects eat.

To further elaborate on the influence of mouthpart structure on insect feeding, let's consider the many beneficial insects that consume a varied diet. How about the mature ladybug whose mouth needs to be able to both grind up aphids and drink nectar? And how about the adult syrphid fly that must lap up nectar as easily as it consumes grains of pollen? Or the teeny, tiny big-eyed bug that can eat small seeds, nectar, and sap when insect prey are hard to come by? The mouthparts of these insects—and all others—have beautifully evolved to suit their needs.

But just as a mouthpart determines an insect's style of eating, so too does its design determine exactly which flowers the insect can access for nectar and pollen. The mouthparts of nectar-feeding beneficial insects are specialized for sure, but there are limitations to their use. They aren't designed, for example, to reach to the bottom of a deep, tubular flower like a butterfly's proboscis. Nor do most beneficial insects have bodies heavy enough to spring open a snapdragon like a bumblebee's body can. For nectar- and pollen-eating beneficial insects, not just any flower will do.

As you'll recall, many beneficial insects require pollen and nectar to live and reproduce.

The caterpillar of the question mark butterfly uses its chewing mouthparts to grind up leaf tissue.

From the beautiful green lacewing and the stalking spider to the tiniest parasitic wasp and the largest tachinid fly, these insects must have access to this plant-based nutrition to do their best work. Different flower shapes influence how available nectar and pollen are to feeding beneficials. Many studies involving syrphid flies show how flower shape relates to mouthpart morphology and diet. What has been discovered is a huge variation among species in the amounts of nectar and pollen consumed, and even in the particular flowers each species likes to visit. This is because even within the syrphid fly family, each species has a different mouthpart; some are short and thick while others are long and slim.

Many beneficial insects aren't as heavy as this bumblebee and therefore are not able to access nectar from flowers like a snapdragon. Instead, beneficial insects rely on flowers that are well suited to both their mouthpart structure and their smaller stature.

Different syrphid fly species have different mouthpart structures. Those with shorter mouthparts, such as this one, tend to eat more pollen and visit more open, exposed flowers (like those of this angelica), while those with longer mouthparts prefer more elongated flowers and drink more nectar.

Species with long, thin mouthparts tend to have a greater portion of nectar in their diet, and those with shorter mouthparts eat more pollen and tend to visit a larger number of open, exposed flowers. Those with longer mouthparts, of course, can more readily access nectar from elongated flowers. But why then did the studied syrphids with longer mouthparts not drink from shallower flowers more often, simply because it was easier to access the nectar? Fascinatingly, flowers with a deeper, more elongated corolla (petal structure) have nectar with a different sugar content, so the flies need to visit fewer flowers to meet their nutritional needs. Wouldn't you work a little harder to get a turkey sandwich than you would to get a piece of lettuce?

what's in nectar and why do certain flowers attract certain bugs?

Before I get into which flower structures are best suited for natural enemies, let's talk nectar. I've been going on and on about how important it is for beneficial insects to have access to it, but I realize I shouldn't assume that every gardener really knows what nectar is. When I called up a Master Gardener friend and asked her what nectar is, she answered, "It's the sugary liquid in a flower that pollinators use for energy." In essence, she's correct. But nectar is far more complicated than that.

Though nectar properties vary greatly, most nectar consists of several different ingredients, including water, sugars, amino acids, lipids, and proteins. The amount of water in any given nectar is dependent on many factors, including genetics, drought stress, and humidity. In general, plants that are drought stressed tend to produce smaller and fewer flowers; thus, less nectar is produced by plants grown in drier conditions. On the other hand, overwatering increases nectar production in certain plants, but this can cause the sugars to be less concentrated, perhaps making them less inviting to some pollinators.

Water levels, however, aren't the only determining factor in nectar sugar content. Depending, too, on a plant's genetics, nectar can contain as little as 2 percent or as much as 75 percent sugar, and there is great variability even within plant families. But plants with similar pollinators tend to have similar nectar sugar concentration—largely related, again, to the mouthpart structure of the pollinating insect. Insects can obtain nectar either by lapping it up or by sucking it up through

Deep, tubular flowers, like those of this crocosmia, are often filled with high-sucrose nectars meant to attract a particular class of pollinators—those with specialized mouthparts able to access the nectar.

a long straw. Nectars with lower concentrations of sugar aren't very thick and can easily be sucked up through the straw, while those that are more concentrated and viscous can be easily lapped up but are difficult to draw through a narrow tube. Warm weather also makes nectar less viscous and probably easier to drink, explaining why insects get higher rewards by feeding in warmer weather.

To make it even more interesting, sugar isn't just sugar. Nectar is a mixture of three primary types of sugar—sucrose, fructose, and glucose—and other minor sugars (sorbitol, xylose, maltose, and others) as well. Most nectars have mixed sugar composition, and the balance remains relatively consistent among individual plants within the same species. The nectar sugar proportions a plant produces attract a particular class of pollinators. An examination of nine hundred different nectars found high-sucrose nectars most often in the more tubular flowers pollinated by bees, butterflies, moths, and hummingbirds, while nectars including those rich in glucose were present in the shallow flowers most often visited by small, unspecialized insects like many beneficials.

Nectar comes from either the plant's phloem or the nectary tissue itself, and the volume and concentration of nectar tend to be inversely proportional. As water evaporates and nectar volume goes down, its sugar concentration goes up. Long, tubular flowers, however, are better at regulating humidity so water evaporates more slowly from these flowers, making the nectar volume higher and the sugar concentration in these blooms lower. What all this means is that some plants offer higher rewards to visiting pollinators in the form of more concentrated or more copious nectar. It's no surprise that these flowers are visited more often.

Also present in nectar are amino acids. The amounts and types present in any given flower also determine which pollinators will be most attracted to it. Certain amino acids attract butterflies while others lure in bees

The amino acids present in any given nectar help determine which pollinators are attracted to the flower; some amino acids attract bees while others draw beetles, moths, or certain beneficial insects. The amino acids present in the nectar of this marigold may have helped lure in a soldier beetle.

or beetles. Different amino acids have different tastes, which may also serve to entice a particular pollinator.

Nectar's other components also play a key role in attracting suitable pollinators. The lipids (fats), proteins, organic acids, and microbes in nectar all serve a purpose. Some are lures, while others make the nectar unpal-

nectar in exchange for pest protection

There is no doubt that, as noted by my Master Gardener friend, nectar serves as a sweet energy reward for pollination—but it also serves as a reward for protection. You see, nectar isn't only produced in flowers. More than sixty different plant families include species that produce nectar in sites other than the flowers. Extrafloral nectar (EFN) is distinguished from floral nectar by the fact that it isn't involved in pollination and is produced via specialized structures.

The extrafloral nectar produced via the specialized structures on this cherry leaf offers a sweet reward to beneficial insects in return for their help controlling herbivorous pests.

atable to unwanted visitors, essentially preventing nectar thievery. Some make the plant smell good or act as a defensive antibiotic against embryo-attacking microorganisms, while others may create a fluorescent trail as a visual cue to pollinators. A few nectars even contain narcotics that make pollinators loiter a bit more within each flower, increasing the chances of successful pollination. And still others include stimulants that encourage pollinators to visit as many flowers as possible, leading to an increase in cross-pollination. Talk about a nicotine and caffeine buzz!

This nectar was first thought to just be a way for a plant to excrete metabolic wastes, but we now know that plants use EFN to attract predators and parasitoids by offering them a reward for helping to control herbivorous pests. Thousands of different plant species—including nearly every type of plant: herbs, shrubs, trees, vines, annuals, and perennials—produce EFN. The structures that produce EFN can be located on the leaves, petioles (leaf stalks), fruits, or other plant parts, and they are often situated where insects can easily access them by either crawling or flying.

The composition of EFN is different from that of floral nectar. It's about 95 percent sugars and 5 percent amino acids, lipids, and other components. It is known to be a suitable food source for a large range of insect species; it is not, however, a complete source of nutrition and therefore makes beneficial insects *need* to feed on protein sources (like pest insects!) to fill in the nutritional gaps.

A study that examined the EFN of lima beans to determine its role in attracting predators and parasitoids determined that parasitic wasp and fly species were significantly increased when artificial EFN was present, and the bean tendrils with artificial EFN present had significantly less pest damage than those without the artificial EFN. You may ask why these researchers had to use artificial EFN for their project. Interestingly, natural EFN is often secreted in conjunction with semio-chemicals, making it difficult to determine whether the parasitoids and predators are coming because of the EFN or because they are receiving the emergency signal from the plant. These researchers, however, only added the artificial EFN in amounts and locations similar to natural EFN production. It was clear in this study that the presence of EFN alone accounted for the increase in predation and parasitism.

Many different insects sip EFN, including a large number of natural enemies, making it a valuable tool in a plant's defensive arsenal. When plants with the ability to excrete EFN are attacked by herbivores, they pump out more of it in hopes of luring in the good guys. EFN serves as an indirect defense against herbivores and can be produced throughout the day and even during the night.

EFN can be produced by members of many common plant families, including Rosaceae (roses, strawberries), Euphorbiaceae (euphorbias, poinsettias), Asteraceae (asters), Liliaceae (lilies), Fabaceae (peas, beans), Curbitaceae (squash, cucumbers, melons), and Asclepiadaceae (milkweed). In my garden I can readily spot EFN production sites on my elderberries, fruit trees, beautyberries, peonies, sunflowers, morning glories, impatiens, and hibiscus. EFN is, in fact, a very important extra nutrient source for natural enemies, especially when prey are scarce. Being on the lookout for EFN production sites on your own plants can lead to some interesting interactions with insects.

As you can see, nectar isn't nearly as simple as we think. Plants know what they are doing. They have evolved to intersect with the insects they rely on in many striking and spectacular ways.

Peonies produce extrafloral nectar on their flower buds. Though ants most commonly reap the benefits, so do certain beneficials. Here a larger species of syrphid fly laps up EFN from around the base of the bud.

some plants have it and some don't

Now that you know how the structure of an insect's mouth influences its feeding, as well as how any given nectar can be either enticing or averting to a particular insect, it's time to acknowledge the fact that some flowers have it and some don't. The *it* I am referring to is the critical combination of flower architecture and nectar composition and yumminess that natural enemies find appealing. Only the insects know which flowers work with their mouths and which ones provide the best nectar for them; we can merely make our best guess as to which plants fit the bill. Taste testing different nectars ourselves is out of the question for many obvious reasons, so instead we turn to a plant's floral architecture to guide us to those plants that our predators and parasitoids might be drawn to.

As I mentioned earlier, different flower shapes and sizes influence how available their nectar and pollen is to feeding benefi-cials based on their varied body sizes and mouthparts. For example, smaller parasitoids (remember, some of them are not even as big as a gnat) often seek out the open, exposed nectaries of tiny, shallow flowers. The exposure of the nectaries is very important—they can be fully exposed, partially exposed, or fully concealed. Larger beneficials may have the ability to push their way into a flower to access the nectar from a concealed nectary, but smaller ones certainly do not. In most cases, plants that produce a lot of small flowers with exposed nectaries are the most user friendly to the largest diversity of beneficial insects.

Scores of studies have examined which plant families are most attractive to natural enemies, and I used information gleaned from these studies to compile the list of plants

Tiny parasitoids, like the minuscule parasitic wasps on this dill, require exposed nectaries and shallow flowers to access nectar. Open nectaries, such as those present in members of the carrot family (Apiaceae), are among the most user friendly to the largest diversity of beneficial insects.

profiled in the next chapter. For example, beginning in 2003, researchers at Michigan State University compared different native plant species to determine which appealed to the largest diversity of beneficial insects. They collected and identified every predator, parasitoid, and pollinator they found and discovered which plants were the most attractive. This type of information is meant to steer us toward the best plants for our insectary borders. We know that having these food sources available increases the longevity and reproductive capability of these insects. We also know without a doubt that the presence of flowering plants increases the rates of parasitism and predation. Knowing which plants attract which predators and parasitoids enables gardeners to increase the diversity of natural enemies in their gardens.

In another study, begun in 1928 and lasting thirty-three years, researchers documented more than fifteen thousand insect parasitoids present on several hundred different plant species in central Illinois to examine what kinds of plants attract what kinds of insect visitors. They found that the plants with the most parasitic wasp species present were members of the carrot family (Apiaceae)—with an average of twelve parasitic wasp species per plant species! Other important plant families for these parasitoids were the aster family (Asteraceae), the spurge family (Euphorbiaceae), the pea and bean family (Fabaceae), and several others. The carrot family is so important to parasitoids because members of this family have those open, exposed nectaries. The other plant families frequented by parasitoids had more concealed nectaries and so were found to be more attractive to certain wasp families but not others. The ten plant species that hosted the largest diversity of parasitic wasp species offered nectar that was easily accessed by wasps with all sorts of different mouthparts.

good for bugs versus good in gardens

Studies like these, and many others, do in fact tell us which plants are most attractive to beneficials, but they don't necessarily tell us which plants are gardenworthy. For example, poison or spotted hemlock (*Conium maculatum*), a native of Europe, and a similar North American species, spotted water hemlock (*Cicuta maculata*), are both exceedingly appealing to beneficial insects of all sorts. They are found across the entire North American continent, but both are incredibly poisonous to humans and livestock, making them a very bad selection for the insectary border (just ask Socrates—he was executed by being forced to drink a concoction of poison hemlock). Both plants are also considered noxious invasive weeds in many regions. However, these species are very valuable nectar and pollen sources for numerous beneficial insects and—even though you probably don't want them in your yard or garden—a roadside patch can provide food for many beneficials.

Not all of the plants known to be attractive to nectar-seeking beneficial insects belong in the garden. Some of them, including this poison hemlock (*Conium maculatum*), are considered noxious invasive weeds and are poisonous to humans and livestock. Still, this patch up the street from my house harbors a plethora of beneficials, shown on the next page.

Spined soldier bug eggs

Rove beetle

Seven-spotted ladybug

Syrphid fly

Ladybug larva

Wild parsnip (*Pastinaca sativa*), a European introduction, is highly attractive to many beneficial insects but can cause a rash if plant juices contact the skin. While wild populations support many different beneficials, planting it in your garden isn't a good idea.

Another North American native plant, the common cow parsnip (*Heracleum maximum*, also called *H. lanatum*), also bears flowers that are highly attractive to beneficials, but contact with the plant's leaves and stems can cause a rash. Though cow parsnip is considered a noxious weed in some states, others list it as threatened. Personally, I like this plant—I think it's bold and beautiful. But I sure-as-shootin' don't want to touch it. The same is true for the wild parsnip (*Pastinaca sativa*). It carries a similar appeal to beneficial insects, but this European introduction can also cause a terrible rash if skin comes in contact with the juices and is then exposed to bright sun. And it's on the noxious weed list for several states as well. While I wouldn't suggest you add either of these plants to your insectary border, letting wild patches remain does serve to help support many natural enemies.

Other plants are certainly on the "harmful to humans but attractive to natural enemies" list, including certain cowbanes (some *Oxypolis* species and *Cicuta virosa*, which is also called Mackenzie's, or northern, water hemlock). So while scientific studies might reveal the best plants for supporting beneficial insects, they don't necessarily reveal the best plants for insectary gardens. The plants I have chosen to include in the next chapter are known to lure beneficials and are also exemplary garden specimens. They are beautiful and useful—and the complex landscape they

help to create supports higher parasitism and predation rates. As you'll see, some of these plants may already be at home in your garden; the list includes several common herbs and cut flowers, as well as everyday perennials and annuals. It's clear that these plants need to serve not only our resident natural enemies but also the people living there.

a word on native plants

Reviewing reports and research on the benefits of native plants for good bug populations is both revealing and confusing. Admittedly, it is a bit difficult to separate fact from conjecture when it comes to using native plants to attract beneficial insects to any particular landscape. While it surely would seem that native plants have more to offer our native beneficial insects in terms of presenting them with the proper floral architecture and nectar rewards, it's a point that continues to be studied, and even debated, by many scientists across North America and around the world.

I don't think many would argue the point that our native beneficial insects are more familiar with our native plant species, having been born and bred together for tens of thousands of years. Without a doubt, the two share a lot of history. Surely the good bugs recognize these plants more readily, but does that mean native plants have more to offer and are visited more frequently than introduced species?

Are the North American native plants found in this garden better able to attract and support our native nectar-seeking beneficials? It's a point that continues to be studied and even debated.

Telling you all this puts me in a very tight spot. You see, I want you to plant native plants in your insectary border—but it isn't necessarily because I can prove that they are more attractive to the beneficial insects living there. It's because I believe in the goodness of them. Native plant advocates rightfully sing the praises of using native plant species in the landscape, and they are, in my opinion, correct in stressing that natives are better adjusted to local growing conditions and less likely to take over the garden and upset the balance of the natural plant communities around them. It's generally agreed that native plants are also more valuable to our native bees, and certain native plants serve as essential larval food for our butterfly and moth species. For many insects, native plants are necessities.

That being said, many of the plants commonly recommended for luring in beneficial insects are nonnative species. And although I would much prefer you select a variety of native plants for your insectary border, I would be remiss if I didn't point out the fitness of several nonnative plants as nectar sources for many natural enemies. And that is why you'll find the plant profiles in the coming chapter to be a mixture of a few nonnative species whose beneficial-luring prowess has been well documented, and a substantial number of North American native plants. It is possible to have an insectary border made exclusively of native plants, or one that

Some scientists say yes, and others note it only as speculation. While I would love to say that without a doubt native plant species are better at attracting nectar-seeking beneficial insects, the statement would be without the proper backing; while some studies do indeed show that certain native plants are better at luring in the good guys, others show that several introduced plant species are more attractive to nectar-seeking beneficial insects.

consists of a mixture of native and nonnative species. I'll leave that decision to the gardener.

the wonder of weeds

While plants that have been classified as noxious or invasive weeds in a particular region should not be promoted, many plants that gardeners may consider weeds do provide resources for beneficial insects. Plants like thistle, lamb's quarters, chickweed, clover, and even dandelion are an important food and habitat source for many beneficials. Weeds have always been thought of as the enemy because of their competition with desirable plants. Their presence can certainly result in reduced yields as they compete for light, food, and water; however, weeds also play a huge role in the biology of many beneficial insects by serving as alternate food sources and further diversifying the garden habitat. Earlier in this book I promised that an insectary garden doesn't have to be a weedy mess, and I'm not changing my mind about that. What I want to stress is that wiping out every weed in your landscape is not necessary, or even good.

It's been documented that the presence of certain weeds increases the population of beneficial insects and therefore reduces pest damage. Weedy habitats on farms benefit natural enemies because they also aid in synchronizing good and bad insect populations, provide an excellent source of nectar and pollen, and

Weeds, such as the lamb's quarters shown here, can enhance beneficial bug populations on farms and in gardens. Their flowers can provide beneficials with nectar when prey insects are not yet available, and they can provide alternate insect hosts.

plants, bugs, and weather in sync: the stunning science of insect phenology

Based on an interview with Daniel Herms, PhD, professor of entomology at The Ohio State University, Columbus, Ohio, and co-coordinator of the OSU Phenology Garden Network

FOR FURTHER PROOF of how tightly connected insects and plants are, we can look to the stunning science of phenology. It turns out that life is more predictable than you might think (well, at least plant and insect life). The study of phenology examines recurring plant and animal life-cycle events and their connection to the weather. Phenological events like the blooming of a maple tree, a songbird's spring arrival, the migration of a monarch, and the egg hatch of eastern tent caterpillars are tied to environmental conditions, as nearly all natural phenomena are. Most gardeners have witnessed earlier bud break or faster flowering when the weather is warm, and we know that many insects show up earlier under those same conditions. Both plant and insect development are intimately connected to temperature. This is because plants and insects don't use clocks but instead use the conditions of their environment to keep time. The scientists who study the natural sequence of these events have discovered that phenological events track time with amazing predictability and accuracy.

Daniel Herms has been interested in phenology since the 1980s, when he began to monitor flower and insect phenology as a tool to predict pest insect activity. He points out that many phenological events in the plant world correspond with the appearance of particular insects. For example, in Ohio black vine weevil adults emerge just a few days after the American yellowwood tree reaches full bloom, the eggs of eastern tent caterpillars hatch just as the first forsythia flower opens, and greater peach tree borers emerge as adults when the northern catalpa tree begins to flower. Interestingly, the phenological sequence in one region often shows few deviations from that in nearby regions containing the same plant and insect species; and the phenological order remains the same even when weather conditions differ. In warmer springs, phenological events may be advanced by a few weeks, but they still happen in the same chronological order.

All these indicators serve as a sort of biological calendar that humans were once intimately connected with. "I think of phenology as the foundational science of human existence," says Herms, "because it's the foundation of

The blooming of a maple tree is a pheno-logical event—a natural phenomenon tied to environmental conditions. Plant and insect development are inexorably linked to weather and temperature.

agriculture. Agriculture is so tied to the rhythm of nature, as are our own lives, even though we don't think about it so much anymore. Older civilizations were obsessed with phenology because they couldn't survive without these predictors. They couldn't just reach for their cell phone; instead, they used a natural succes-sion of events to track the passage of time and predict what would come next."

Because plants and insects are such precise timekeepers, recorded emergence dates can tell us a lot about changes in both long- and short-term weather patterns. Herms notes that a look at the recorded emergence dates and life cycles of many insects in the Northern Hemisphere reveal several concerns. One is that some insects are showing up where they haven't been seen before, mostly moving north;

for example, the southern pine beetle is now in Ohio, and bagworms are now a major pest in northern Ohio when they used to occur only in the southern part of the state. In addition, some insects that used to produce only one generation per year are now producing two. Another concern is that insect emergence times have changed over the past thirty to forty years; many insects are emerging significantly earlier than they did in the 1970s, creating a challenge for pest management. Many phenological events in temperate climates have advanced two and a half days per decade since 1971; thus, the seasonal development of plants and animals has advanced by about ten days in four decades. "This change, of course, coincides with the fact that the world is getting warmer," says Herms. "The phenological records kept for many years by numerous scientists around the world provide very valuable information for tracking climate change. There's no doubt that our warming climate is affecting insects."

"Though changes in life cycles and distribution are big concerns, another potential problem is the decoupling of phenological synchronization," adds Herms. "Plants and insects interact closely and if they respond differently to climate change, then the timing of when the insect is active versus when the plant is flowering could get disrupted." Obviously, this could have ecological consequences, but the data seems to be mixed so far, with some scientists finding that plant and insect phenologies are changing together and others showing a decoupling of plant and insect species. Then there's what's known as the phenological window hypothesis, which proposes that an insect may need to feed on a host plant at a specific time in the plant's development for the best nutritional conditions. If these don't sync, there could be repercussions.

Climate change has many cascading effects on insect and other animal life. One example Herms provides is that of the mountain pine beetle. This western pest has moved up into northern Alberta and British Columbia, where it is devastating lodgepole pine forests in areas where it has never existed before. In the Rocky Mountains of Colorado and Wyoming, it is moving to higher altitudes, where it is having a similar impact on whitebark pines—whose nuts are a critical food of grizzly bears. The grizzlies consequently have had to forage at lower altitudes, resulting in more human-grizzly interactions, and have been going into hibernation at lower weights.

Soon after Herms came to The Ohio State University, he and county extension agent Denise Ellsworth decided to devise a way to track phenological events across Ohio. This would allow them to examine how climactic variation within the state was affecting insects and plants, and to confirm that the pattern of phenological events in one part of the state was occurring in the same order elsewhere. They also wanted to engage people in citizen science and increase awareness of phenology and its importance to gardeners. Ellsworth began a Master Gardener specialization program in entomology with part of the program focused on plant and insect phenology. She started to develop a network of more than thirty gardens across Ohio in the early 2000s to examine and record plant phenology across the state. All the gardens grow the same plants, and Master Gardener volunteers have collected phenological data, which a graduate student has compiled and entered into a website at www.oardc.ohio-state.edu/gdd/. Ohio residents can enter their zip codes and receive a list of all the phenological events occurring in their area based on locally recorded weather conditions and temperatures. They can also look up events in past years as a comparison.

The cascading effects of climate change are illustrated by the case of the mountain pine beetle, whose range has expanded to higher altitudes in the Rockies where it is now killing whitebark pines. The grizzlies that feed on pine nuts have begun to forage at lower altitudes, putting them in more frequent contact with humans, and are hibernating at lower weights.

Other organizations also use citizen science to record phenological events. Organizations like the U.S.A. National Phenology Network (www.usanpn.org), the Leopold Phenology Project (www.aldoleopold.org), and Project BudBurst (www.neoninc.org/budburst) invite gardeners across North America to join them in collecting phenological observations. You can sign on with one or more of them and help make a difference.

"Gardeners have had an intimate relationship with insects for thousands and thousands of years," says Herms. "For many of those years, people were gardening with insects, and I suppose it's merely a tiny blip of geologic time between when chemical insecticides were invented and now. We are beginning to see insects again and to pay attention to them. We're getting reacquainted with them and are now interested in butterfly and pollinator gardens and phenology. . . . There's been an enlightenment about the role of insects in ecology and about gardens as havens for diversity. And all of that is very good."

help increase the number of available species. Weed nectar sources fill in important gaps, when prey or host insects are not yet available and when the favored insectary plants are not in bloom.

Having some weeds around is just good for business. One study described "spectacular parasitism rates" in an apple orchard that was interplanted with a blend of flowering weeds. Another found that parasitism of tent caterpillars and codling moths was eighteen times higher in orchards with flowering weedy undergrowth than in those with few weeds. A third discovered that two species of cabbage worms were parasitized 50 percent more when particular flowering weeds were grown nearby.

Weeds also provide beneficial insects with alternate hosts. A species of tachinid fly, for example, can use a ragweed stalk borer as a host when its preferred host, the European corn borer, is not available. Ragweed, as a matter of fact, is shown to support many alternative hosts and therefore to increase parasitism rates of the desired target pest. The same can be said of smartweed, pigweed, stinging nettle, lamb's quarters, goldenrod, and other plants commonly thought of as weeds. Weeds also bring more prey insects like aphids and mites; this could lead you to believe that their presence means beneficials might prefer to visit them and eat their associated pests rather then gobble down the aphids in your lettuce,

but most of the time this isn't the case. All that extra prey means more reproduction, a greater chance of survival, and improved parasitism rates. However, in some situations, particularly on farms, natural enemies do prefer to stay in sheltered weedy habitats rather than moving into open fields. Some farmers solve this problem by timing the mowing of weed habitats to force predatory insects to move into crop fields and orchards when they are most needed.

The trick, of course, comes in the balance. How many weeds are too many? You don't want them to outcompete desirable plants, nor do you want to have a completely weed-free landscape and miss a terrific opportunity to increase good bug populations. The balance comes from picking your battles. Avoid encouraging weeds with running root systems that can quickly overtake the landscape (bindweed, Canada thistle, and Japanese knotweed are examples), keep weeds from going to seed by timing mowings appropriately, and don't eliminate each and every weed from your lawn. Clover, speedwell, chickweed, dandelions, and other weeds aren't necessarily the enemy.

But here is the quandary gardeners like me face in regard to our weeds and their benefits to good bugs: what if I just don't like the way they look? As a horticulturist, I don't like a messy garden. I weed regularly and try to keep my garden beds as weed free as possible (the lawn, however, is a different story—I could care less what grows in there as long as it's semi-green). When I began to look at ways to encourage my good bugs without resorting to the jungle look, I discovered that many of the benefits of weeds are also found in an insectary border, with or without weeds in it.

When you design your own insectary border, you decide what to plant in it—and if your plans include no weeds, that's OK. If, on the other hand, you want to let your border get a little wild and weedy, that's OK too. In a way, insectary borders are meant to be a substitute of sorts for the weedy habitats we gardeners often feel we should discourage. They provide the same benefits in regard to habitat, food, and prey for natural enemies. But to really do good by your beneficials, why not have both? Plant a beautiful, lively insectary border filled to the brim with exciting and enticing plants, and also relax your anti-weed morals and let some of them be.

plant profiles

the best plants for beneficials

The beautiful and diverse plants in this insectary border support insect life that is integral to the health and balance of the entire landscape. Though you needn't cover your entire front yard with insectary plantings, doing so is a gorgeous idea.

part of my job as co-host of a radio program called *The Organic Gardeners* is to answer questions from callers about how to get rid of bugs. This never used to be a problem for me; I would tell the caller what organic product to spray to get rid of the perceived pest, and that would be that. But now that I am a confessed bug lover it's a different story, and I struggle to find a balance. I want to go into a long, involved elucidation of how callers are gardening wrong and how they need to appreciate their bugs and how everything is connected, but if I did they would probably hang up on me. I hear the "just tell me what to spray" tone in their voice. So instead of giving a lecture, I tell

them not to panic. Seldom does an insect actually kill a plant in a garden setting. Yes, the plant might not look so good for a while, but the chances of its survival are excellent. I then suggest a preventive measure they can employ for the following season and sometimes offer them an organic product solution.

My favorite times are when I get the opportunity to tell the caller that I haven't sprayed a single plant in my own garden with any insecticides (organic or otherwise) in about ten years. My radio co-host can claim that he has not sprayed for nearly twenty years. Over the years I have come to know my bugs, and I know how tolerant my plants are of them. That being said, it is also very seldom that I actually have a major pest outbreak in my landscape anymore. My garden is very stable. And it's so stable because it is so diverse.

This chapter will help you get started on building your insect-friendly landscape by describing some of the best plants for natural enemies. These plants are top-notch providers of the accessible food and habitat beneficial insects need to feel welcome and content. Many of these plants produce flowers with small, accessible nectaries, which as you may recall from the previous chapter are the most user friendly to the widest assortment of beneficials. Choose a diverse mixture of plants with differing floral architectures, bloom times, and growth habits, and watch a place of beauty become a garden teeming with insect life.

the importance of landscape diversity and complexity for good bugs

Based on an interview with Paula Shrewsbury, PhD, associate professor of entomology and extension specialist at the University of Maryland, College Park, Maryland

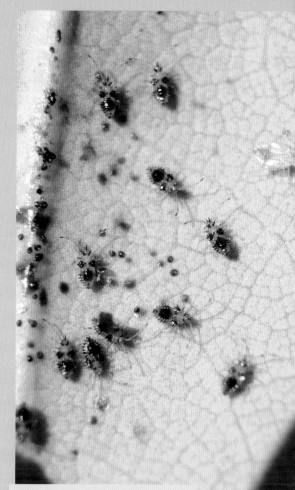

BOTH LANDSCAPE DIVERSITY and complexity are important for good bugs. Diversity refers to the number of different plant species present, while complexity refers to the assortment of growth habits and structures of those plants. According to research conducted by Paula Shrewsbury and her colleagues at the University of Maryland, vegetative diversity and structural complexity in a landscape create a more favorable environment for natural enemies so that they are then better able to control potential pests.

In her PhD research, Shrewsbury studied the azalea lace bug, a pest that causes damage to the leaves of azaleas and rhododendrons. She compared the number of insects in two different kinds of urban landscapes—diverse and simple. There were fewer lace bugs in the diverse landscape, and she found that the

Azalea lace bugs are typically not problematic on azaleas growing in unmanaged forested areas, but in urban and suburban settings, their population levels can get very troublesome. The structural complexity of the forested areas creates more favorable conditions for natural enemies and allows them to better control this pest.

difference in pest numbers was the result of the habitat itself. "There were more beneficial insects in the diverse landscape in terms of both their numbers and the diversity of their species," says Shrewsbury. "The less diverse landscapes supported fewer natural enemies and were therefore more prone to pest outbreaks." It seems that the more vegetation layers there are, the more attractive the environment is to natural enemies. Surprisingly, the ground cover and tree layers seem to be the most important.

One study Shrewsbury and her colleagues conducted involved creating beds of flowering plants on a golf course. The study used plants that have been shown to attract a diversity of beneficial insects—sweet alyssum, coreopsis, and switch grass. These three plants create a somewhat complex environment in that the sweet alyssum is low to the ground, the coreopsis is a bit taller and blooms later in the season, and the switch grass is a bunching grass that is attractive to ground-based predators like ground beetles. "We aimed for continuous bloom and diverse floral architecture, and then added the habitat of the grasses," Shrewsbury explains. What they found was an increase in pest predation over an area extending out from those beds by nearly 40 feet (12 meters).

Shrewsbury suggests that homeowners consider examining the same elements in their own yards—flower structure, shape, bloom time, and habitat creation—to create more sustainable landscape systems that are less prone to pest outbreaks. "Landscapes with more structural complexity have more insects in general; as a result, their species richness is greater and there are more prey items available for the natural enemies. Habitat with more prey supports more natural enemies. They can then prevent pest outbreaks."

The landscape complexity Paula Shrewsbury champions is essential to encouraging your good bugs. You don't have to rip up every inch of lawn (but if you really want to, go right ahead), nor do you have to change everything about your existing garden. "A lot of home landscapes already have some diversity as far as trees and shrubs are concerned, but when you add more, look to diversify those plant species," she advises. She suggests these three steps to creating a beneficials-friendly landscape: first, choose plants that thrive in your climate; second, select plants known to support natural enemies (you'll learn about a whole bunch of them in this chapter); and third, work to increase the structural complexity of your yard.

Common yarrow (*Achillea millefolium*) bears white flowers in a flat-topped structure that lasts for weeks in the garden.

• •

Achillea millefolium
common yarrow, milfoil

FAMILY Asteraceae (aster)

- perennial, USDA zones 3–8
- North American native with many native and introduced subspecies and varieties
- blooms spring to summer
- 2–3 feet (0.6–1.0 m) high and as wide

Common yarrow is widely distributed across North America, and the straight species is now so prevalent that it is considered an invasive weed in many regions. There are numerous subspecies, varieties, and cultivars of this plant, and it's often difficult to determine the nativeness of any particular selection. *Achillea millefolium* bears white flowers while its cultivars range in color from pink to purple, red, and yellow. Both the straight species and its cultivars bear hairy, feathery, lance-shaped leaves that are distinctly fragranced. Its many small flowers are combined into a flat-topped flower structure (inflorescence) with each individual bloom organized like all members of the aster family: a group of central disk flowers surrounded by several colorful ray flowers bearing a strap-shaped corolla that appears as a petal. Yarrow is a favorite of lacewings, ladybugs, syrphid flies, parasitic wasps, damsel bugs, and others.

The dense mat of lacy foliage produced by yarrow before the flower stalks arrive is one of my favorite early-season garden

Syrphid flies are among the many beneficials that benefit from the presence of common yarrow.

textures. The flattened inflorescence is long lasting and provides weeks of color in the garden, but with its top-heavy structure the plant may require staking, particularly if sited in less than full sun. Common yarrow is drought tolerant.

Other insectary species: *Achillea filipendulina*, or fern-leaf yarrow, is also a welcome sight to many beneficials. It is a European introduction that bears densely packed, flat-topped flower clusters in a brilliant golden

Lacewing larvae enjoy foraging for prey among the flowers of fern-leaf yarrow.

Fern-leaf yarrow (*Achillea filipendulina*) is a European introduction that is also a welcome sight to many beneficials.

yellow. The foliage is gray-green and slightly fuzzy. It, too, provides a long season of color with flower clusters that can reach a hearty 5 inches (13 cm) across. By midsummer, the flowers of the fern-leaf yarrow growing in a friend's garden host numerous minute pirate bugs. The insects tuck themselves between the tiny flowers. Brushing the flower tops gently with a hand brings them scurrying across the surface where they are easily seen—even without a hand lens.

• •

Ammi majus

bishop's flower, false Queen Anne's lace, laceflower, lady's lace, bullwort

FAMILY Apiaceae (carrot)

- annual
- native to parts of Europe and the Middle East
- blooms late summer through fall
- 2 feet (0.6 m) high, 1 foot (0.3 m) wide

I'll refer to *Ammi majus* as laceflower to avoid confusion with bishop's weed and true Queen Anne's lace, about which I'll say more in a moment. Laceflower thrives in full to partial sun and requires little more than average garden soil with a dose of organic matter. Because it is an annual, you should plan to plant new seeds each spring, though in many situations laceflower readily self-sows. Its flower clusters reach 4 to 5 inches (10–13 cm) across and are welcoming to parasitic wasps, minute pirate bugs, big-eyed bugs, syrphid flies, ladybugs, lacewings, and other beneficials.

Other insectary species: A sister species, *Ammi visnaga*, is known as toothpickweed and bears similar flowers but has lacier foliage. Its wide clusters of tiny white flowers are highly appealing to many species of beneficials.

In the same family as *Ammi majus* and to some extent attractive to beneficial insects are the common roadside weed known as Queen Anne's lace or wild carrot (*Daucus carota*) and the perennial ground cover known as bishop's weed (*Aegopodium podagraria*). All three

Laceflower (*Ammi majus*) is an annual that readily self-sows. Each flower cluster can reach 5 inches (13 cm) across and is attractive to many species of natural enemies.

bear umbrella-shaped clusters of tiny white flowers. But bishop's weed is highly invasive and nearly impossible to eradicate without a backhoe, making it a very bad idea for the garden. True Queen Anne's lace is often listed as a recommended plant for luring in beneficials, but this is a controversial recommendation. The plant, from which all edible carrots were cultivated, is a native of Europe that has naturalized in every part of the continental United States and Canada, a biennial whose seeds are readily dispersed. Its tough nature makes it perfectly suited to disturbed sites, but it is now listed as a noxious weed in several states and the sale and import of its seeds are prohibited in others. *Ammi majus* and *D. carota* were found to attract an equal number

Ammi visnaga is known as toothpick-weed. Its lacy foliage is covered with wide clusters of tiny white flowers that are highly appealing to many species of beneficials.

of minute pirate bugs in field studies, so I suggest you introduce *A. majus* to your insectary border and leave the *D. carota* next to the semis on the interstate.

One last option: for those who plan to construct an insectary garden of natives only, cow parsnip (*Heracleum maximum*, syn. *H. lanatum*) is another alternative. Though I mentioned this native species in the previous chapter's section on "dangerous to humans but attractive to natural enemies" for its ability to cause a rash with skin contact, it has the same white umbrella-shaped flowers as both laceflower and true Queen Anne's lace. It is, however, a far larger plant in both height and girth.

● ●

Anethum graveolens
dill

FAMILY Apiaceae (carrot)

- annual
- native to the Mediterranean region and parts of Asia Minor
- blooms midsummer through fall
- 1–2 feet (0.3–0.6 m) high, 1 foot (0.3 m) wide

The sole species in the genus *Anethum*, dill is a ubiquitous plant in gardens across North America. The delicate, finely dissected leaves are a delightful blue-green, and the diminutive yellow flowers are organized into umbels that can reach 6 or more inches (15 or more cm) across and open from the outside in. Along with other members of its family, dill plays host to the larvae of black swallowtail butterflies, and its blossoms are animated with

The flower clusters of dill (*Anethum graveolens*) are highly attractive to smaller natural enemies as they can readily access the nectar.

If you are worried that dill may become invasive in your garden, consider planting a native variety of yampah (*Perideridia* species) instead.

insects of all sorts, including tachinid flies, syrphid flies, lacewings, parasitic wasps of all shapes and sizes, ladybugs, damsel bugs, and small bees by the bazillion.

Dill's culinary uses are many and it is easily started from seed (both intentionally and not). It readily self-sows and reaches 2 feet (0.6 m) tall in just a few short weeks. Sited in full sun, dill does not require staking, but in partial shade, plan to support it.

Other insectary species: Because it has naturalized across much of North America, dill has created some apprehension about it becoming invasive. If this concerns you, consider planting North American native

perennial *Perideridia americana*—commonly known as wild dill, thicket parsley, or yampah—instead. A native of the Midwest over to Oklahoma, down to Alabama, and up to Michigan, wild dill is another member of the carrot family and bears umbels of small white flowers. A similar species, *P. gairdneri* (gardener's yampah), is a native of western North America. Both plants reach only 2 to 3 feet (0.6 to 1.0 m) tall and have very finely dissected, slender green leaves. The flowering period is a mere two weeks, and *P. americana* then goes dormant after flowering. There are other, less-common regional species of *Perideridia* that also serve natural enemies of all sorts.

Angelica species

angelica

FAMILY Apiaceae (carrot)

- perennial or biennial, depending on the species; USDA zones 4–7
- many species are North American natives; others are not
- blooms in summer
- 3–9 feet (1–2.75 m) high, 2–4 feet (0.6–1.25 m) wide

Angelica is a bold and beautiful garden plant that prefers full to partial sun and moist soils. It produces massive, hollow flower stalks with large umbrella-shaped clusters of small white to green flowers. Several dozen species of angelica exist, with numerous native selec-

The flowers of purplestem angelica (*Angelica atropurpurea*) are attractive to many beneficials.

Angelica gigas, an introduced species, bears beautiful purple flower heads.

tions occurring throughout North America. The most widespread native species in the eastern United States and Canada is *Angelica atropurpurea* (purplestem angelica), with *A. venenosa* (hairy angelica) being a close second. There are many other North American native angelicas besides, including *A. arguta* in the West and *A. pinnata* in the mountain states. Several nonnative species are common garden plants as well, including *A. archangelica* (commonly called archangel) and the striking, purple-flowered *A. gigas*.

Though the nonnative species are often more readily found in the nursery trade, the native selections are worth seeking out—

especially because they are readily recognized as a nectar source by our native beneficials. If you can't find the native species as plants, know that angelica is reasonably easy to start by direct seeding in the garden in the fall. When started from seed, angelica can take a good four to five years to produce a flower, but when it does, it will knock your socks off. And it will attract hordes of parasitic wasps, minute pirate bugs, ladybugs, syrphid flies, tachinid flies, and others.

The bad news about angelica is that once it struts its flowery stuff, it bites the dust, relying on the seeds it has dispersed to create future generations. This trait is seen by many gardeners as a downside to growing angelica, but when you see how many beneficial insects, bees, and butterflies rely on its nectar, you'll see why it's such a treasured plant for the insectary border.

This dried angelica flower head is playing host to numerous aphids—and a polished ladybug (*Cycloneda munda*) is having them for breakfast.

For many years I wanted an angelica in my own garden, and when I finally got one a few years back, I thought I was purchasing the native purplestem angelica (*Angelica atropurpurea*) because that's what the pot tag stated. But when I got it home, I noticed a different label on the side of the pot. It said *Angelica pachycarpa*—a native of New Zealand. I planted it anyway, thinking that my beneficials would still find it appealing. A year later it finally produced a flower stalk, and although I was prepared for it to be loaded with beneficials, just like the stand of purplestem angelica at our local park, I saw only a small handful of syrphid flies. I can't say for sure that it's because my good bugs didn't recognize this foreign plant, but that's my best guess. As a result, I didn't let the plant drop seed, and I'm now looking forward to planting a properly labeled purplestem angelica in its place.

● ●

Anthemis tinctoria

golden marguerite, golden chamomile

SYNONYM *Cota tinctoria*

FAMILY Asteraceae (aster)

- short-lived perennial, USDA zones 3–7; somewhat cultivar dependent
- native to the Mediterranean region
- blooms mid to late summer
- 1–3 feet (0.3–1.0 m) high and as wide

Golden marguerites are a ray of sunshine. The dazzling yellow, daisylike, 1-inch (2.5 cm) flowers this plant produces light up the garden come midsummer. And their highly fragranced, lacy foliage isn't bad either. The leaf undersides are covered in fine, downy hairs, giving them a dusty gray appearance when flipped over. Though golden marguerites are a short-lived perennial, they kindly self-sow and are easy enough to start from leaf or root cuttings as well as divisions. The many available cultivars include 'Charme', a dwarf selection; and 'Kelwayi', a personal favorite.

Golden marguerites (*Anthemis tinctoria*) are short-lived perennials with sunny yellow flowers and gray-green foliage.

Marguerites host numerous beneficials, including this soldier beetle.

Roman chamomile is another great selection for the insectary border. Here, nectar and pollen from its blossoms are nourishing a syrphid fly.

You'll find syrphid flies, lacewings, ladybugs, parasitic wasps, and tachinid flies regularly visiting the flowers.

Other insectary species: Two other members of the genus *Anthemis* are worth mentioning as possible additions to the insectary border. *Anthemis nobilis* (syn. *Chamaemelum nobile*), known as Roman or English chamomile, is a perennial that bears half-inch (1.27-cm) flowers with yellow centers and white petals. It reaches only 8 to 10 inches (20–25 cm) high and has finely serrated leaves. *Anthemus cotula*, commonly known as wild chamomile, dog fennel, or mayweed, is yet another option, though it is an annual and has distinctly fragranced foliage (read: stinky!). It reaches 1 to 2 feet (0.3–0.6 m) high.

• •

Aurinia saxatilis

basket of gold, gold dust, golden alyssum, golden-tuft alyssum, rock madwort

FAMILY Brassicaceae (cabbage)

- perennial, USDA zones 4–9, with some cultivars hardy to zone 3
- native to Europe
- blooms early to mid spring
- 4–12 inches (10–30 cm) high, 1–2 feet (0.3–0.6 m) wide

This pretty little perennial fills the spring garden with its cheery yellow flowers. Because it flowers so early in the season, basket of gold is also a significant nectar source for early-emerging beneficials, such as syrphid flies, big-eyed bugs, and minute pirate bugs. Evergreen mounds of gray-green foliage are smothered in globes of tiny brilliant gold flowers for several weeks each spring (*Aurinia* = "golden" and *saxatilis* = "growing among the rocks"). The seeds that are produced

shortly thereafter readily germinate come fall, creating a naturalized stand of plants. Because basket of gold requires good drainage and prefers sandy soils, I have mine placed at the top of a stone retaining wall that is back-filled with gravel. Be sure to position this plant in a well-drained area, in a rock garden, or on a slope where its roots will never sit in water. With the proper siting, a colony of basket of gold is readily started from nursery-grown plants. It's also easily started from fall-sown seeds or vegetative cuttings.

Basket of gold also dislikes hot, humid weather and because of this it is often grown as an annual in southern regions. But don't let these two particulars stop you from growing this plant. It is a delightful addition to the insectary garden, and its many positives far outweigh the minimal fuss-factor issues. Many cultivars of this plant are commonly found in the nursery trade. Some even bear white, cream, or lemon yellow blooms.

Basket of gold (*Aurinia saxatilis*) is smothered in rich yellow flowers for several weeks in the early spring.

• •

Baccharis species

baccharis, many species-specific common names

FAMILY Asteraceae (aster)

- evergreen shrub, hardiness varies with species
- North American natives
- blooms spring to fall, depending on species
- varies with species

Eastern baccharis (*Baccharis halimifolia*) is also known as the groundsel tree. It grows primarily in coastal regions of the eastern U.S. and bears creamy white flowers that provide nectar for many beneficials and pollinators.

Coyote brush (*Baccharis pilularis*) is a popular western species of baccharis with many subspecies and cultivars. White flowers appear in late summer and are followed by white, fluffy seedpods.

Baccharis is a particularly valuable insectary plant in the western United States, where it is often used in hedgerow plantings on farms to sustain both pollinators and natural enemies, including lacewings, minute pirate bugs, ladybugs, syrphid flies, and parasitic wasps. More than twenty species of baccharis are native to North America, with the large majority of them being southern or western species. All baccharis species are evergreen and dioecious, meaning that each individual plant is either male or female, with male plants generally being used more frequently for insectary plantings and other landscape uses. Most species are drought tolerant and deer resistant, and many have sticky buds and foliage.

Baccharis pilularis, known commonly as coyote brush or chaparral broom, is a western species with subspecies and cultivars that serve as ground covers and others that reach several feet tall. The flowers are small and white and are appealing to a broad number of pollinators and other beneficials. The seedpods that follow bloom are fluffy white wisps. Coyote brush is hardy in USDA zones 7–9.

Baccharis emoryi (syn. *B. salicina*) is a very similar species with equal benefits to natural enemies. It is a native of the Southwest but prefers moist areas and wetlands. An evergreen species that prefers full to partial sun, it is hardy in USDA zones 8–10.

Baccharis halimifolia, eastern baccharis or groundsel tree, is one of a few species indigenous to the eastern United States, where it grows primarily in coastal regions from Florida to New England and west to Texas. It is fully hardy in USDA zones 6–10, and hardy to zone 4 with winter dieback. Late in the season it bears small heads of yellowish white, cotton-like flowers and is a good choice for insectary plantings in coastal areas. It is toxic to live-stock, though, which has caused a problem for ranchers in the Southwest where this plant has been introduced.

Many other regional species of baccharis are well suited to creating insectary habitat. Check with your local extension service for more recommendations.

Boltonia asteroides var. *latisquama* is a late-season bloomer that is native to the Great Plains. The cultivar 'Snowbank' is a favorite of mine for its upright habit and gray-green foliage.

• •

Boltonia asteroides

boltonia, white doll's daisy, starflower, Bolton's aster, false chamomile, false aster, thousand-flowered daisy

FAMILY Asteraceae (aster)

- perennial, USDA zones 4-9
- North American native
- blooms late summer through frost
- 3-4 feet (1-1.25 m) high, 2-4 feet (0.6-1.25 m) wide

Boltonia supports many different beneficials, including this tachinid fly.

One of my favorite perennials for its strong stems and profuse flowering, boltonia is a stalwart plant that continually pleases. The gray-green foliage is an attractive addition to the garden, and the stems seldom require staking if it is grown in full sun. Boltonia also performs fine in partial sun but may require staking in that case. When late summer arrives, the entire plant is smothered in 1-inch (2.5 cm) daisylike flowers. Each blossom has a central core of yellow disk flowers surrounded by a ring of white rays—and the flowers stay in fine form until the season's first frost. Boltonia is deer resistant and drought tolerant, too. In my garden, I find it swimming with natural enemies far later than nearly any other plant. Tachinid flies, soldier beetles, syrphid flies, minute pirate bugs, ladybugs, big-eyed bugs, and many other beneficials are all regulars on my boltonia.

The small flowers of calamint (*Calamintha* species) appear in midsummer. The fragrance of its foliage is a mixture of mint and oregano.

Calamintha species

calamint

SYNONYMS *Satureja, Clinopodium*

FAMILY Lamiaceae (mint)

- perennial, USDA zones 5–9, though some native species are less hardy
- some species are native to North America while others are native to the Mediterranean and Eurasia
- blooms midsummer to fall
- 1–2 feet (0.3–0.6 m) high and as wide

The calamints are poster children for nomenclature issues—sorting them could be a full-time job for taxonomists. Though *Calamintha* is a frequently used genus for this group of plants, you'll also come across *Satureja* and *Clinopodium* in reference to them. Crazy nomenclature aside, this genus comprises some very valuable insectary species. Calamint is a culinary herb used in Middle Eastern and Italian cuisine; the fragrance of calamint's foliage is a cross between mint and oregano. Because of this distinctive scent, deer don't seem to like it very much. The beneficials likely to be found in calamint include hoverflies, tachinid flies, lacewings, and others. Certain bees also adore the flowers and find their nectar readily available.

Calamints are downright pretty plants. All form loose, airy mounds of shiny, compact foliage that is covered in whorls of tiny lavender-blue to pale pink, two-lipped flowers

Several cultivars of *Boltonia asteroides* var. *latisquama* (a specific variety indigenous to the Great Plains) are widely available, including 'Snowbank', an introduction from the New England Wildflower Society; 'Pink Beauty', a floppier selection that bears light-pink-petaled flowers; 'Nana', a cultivar of short stature that tops out at only 2 feet (0.6 m); and 'Masbolimket' (trade named Jim Crockett), another 2-foot-tall selection that bears violet flowers. All are terrific garden plants.

Calamintha nepatoides 'White Cloud' bears plenty of airy flower stems and lends a soft, frothy feel to the garden.

would be fewer tiny beneficials utilizing the nectar of the large-flowered species (*Calamintha grandiflora*) simply because the flowers are substantially larger and, therefore, probably less accessible to tiny insects.

● ●

Carum carvi
caraway
SYNONYM *Carum velenovsky*
FAMILY Apiaceae (carrot)
- annual, biennial in USDA zones 3–7
- native to Asia, Europe, and North Africa
- blooms midsummer (winter in the South)
- 2 feet (0.6 m) high, 1 foot (0.3 m) wide

A common ingredient in foods from rye bread to sauerkraut, caraway figures in lots of culinary experiences—but you know that's not the primary reason you'll be growing this seemingly delicate plant, right? Grow it first for its enticing blooms and threadlike foliage, then let it go to seed for the sauerkraut crock.

The shallow flowers of caraway (*Carum carvi*) provide nectar to syrphid flies and many other beneficial insects.

every summer. Though several uncommon species are native to the southern United States, the ones I see most frequently in the nursery trade are introductions from the Old World. Lesser calamint (*Calamintha nepeta*, syn. *C. nepetoides*), large-flowered calamint (*C. grandiflora*), and woodland calamint (*C. sylvatica*, syn. *C. officinalis*, *C. ascendens*, *C. baetica*—see what I mean about crazy nomenclature?) are readily available species. All three also have many subspecies and/or cultivars each, making keeping track of them very confusing indeed. I think they are all lovely specimens, though I'm guessing there

It reseeds quite readily and is a hospitable host to syrphid flies, minute pirate bugs, big-eyed bugs, lacewings, parasitic wasps, and other natural enemies.

Caraway is most often grown as an annual or biennial in northern regions and as a winter annual in the South. Since it doesn't flower until its second year of growth, gardeners in the extreme north (zones 3 and below) may find it doesn't always overwinter. The soft pink or white flowers it bears are small and diminutive, but gathered together they make a striking umbrella-shaped inflorescence (called an umbel) like that characteristic of other members of the carrot family. Caraway's stems are hollow, and the leaves are finely divided and featherlike. The leaves and flowers both have a licorice-like flavor and scent. Caraway has naturalized across much of the northern United States and most of Canada and is even on the noxious weed list for a few states for its potential invasiveness.

Other insectary species: Two other closely related, and visually similar, herbs should also be considered for the insectary border: cumin (*Cuminum cyminum*) and chervil (*Anthriscus cerefolium*). Both are annuals in the carrot family, with the former being prized for its seeds and the latter for its tasty foliage. Both bear umbels of small white flowers and lure the same natural enemies as caraway.

The flowers of lanceleaf coreopsis (*Coreopsis lanceolata*) stand on slender stems and provide nectar and pollen for syrphid flies and other beneficials.

● ●

Coreopsis species
coreopsis, tickseed, calliopsis

FAMILY Asteraceae (aster)

- perennial, USDA zones 3–8; some species variation
- North American natives
- blooms midsummer to fall
- 1–6 feet (0.3–1.8 m) high, 1–3 feet (0.3–1 m) wide

Called tickseed for their buggy-looking seeds, these North American natives may already have a home in your garden. Several dozen species of coreopsis exist, and quite a few of them are common garden perennials. They have become so popular because of their ease of growth, long flowering period, drought tolerance, deer resistance, and all-around good looks. Nearly all coreopsis are attractive to good bugs of all sorts, including minute pirate bugs, parasitic wasps, soldier beetles, syrphid flies, lacewings, and spiders. I'd like to share with you a handful of my favorite species.

Annual tickseed (*Coreopsis tinctora*) bears bicolored flowers and readily self-sows.

Coreopsis lanceolata (syn. *C. crassifolia*), lanceleaf or sand coreopsis, is a beautiful, clump-forming plant that thoughtfully self-sows if the plant is not deadheaded. Golden yellow, 1-inch (2.5 cm) flowers are produced atop slender, naked stems. The leaves are indeed lance-shaped and form a nice mound of foliage on the ground. It is native to nearly all of North America and is suited to a broad range of climatic conditions but prefers full sun and average garden soil.

Coreopsis tinctora, golden tickseed or plains coreopsis, is another nice selection.

This annual tickseed produces slender stems with narrow, needlelike leaves. They branch off at the top to produce several 1-inch (2.5 cm) flowers per stem. The ray flowers are burgundy-brown toward the center and golden yellow on the tips. Plains coreopsis self-sows and does have a tendency to become weedy in some areas, though in my friend's garden it is well behaved.

Coreopsis verticillata, whorled tickseed or threadleaf coreopsis, is an uber-common species in today's gardens. With many cultivars, *C. verticillata* is an eastern native with small,

'Moonbeam' coreopsis is a reliable performer in my garden, where it is in continual flower for much of the summer.

The inch-wide flowers of *Coreopsis tripteris* play host to many beneficials, including this crab spider that has captured an unfortunate pollinator—a green sweat bee (*Agapostemon* species).

• •

Coriandrum sativum

coriander, cilantro, Chinese parsley

FAMILY Apiaceae (carrot)

- annual
- native to southern Europe and North Africa
- blooms spring to fall; winter in zones 9-10
- 2-3 feet (0.6-1 m) high, 1-2 feet (0.3-0.6 m) wide

Cilantro is the common name for the foliage of this plant, while coriander refers to the dried seeds. Both are common ingredients in cuisines across the globe. I consider cilantro to be a love/hate herb. You either love it or you hate it—at least as far as the flavor is concerned. Apparently there's a genetic component to the perceived taste of cilantro, and people on the hate side of the fence taste soap when they pop a sprig of cilantro into their mouths. My husband is in that camp. I, however, am on the love side. (This makes for interesting "Mexican night" meals at our house.)

The foliage of cilantro/coriander is highly variable, with broadly lobed leaves gracing the bottom of the plant and highly dissected

narrow leaves and yellow flowers. 'Moonbeam' and 'Zagreb' are two common cultivars.

Coreopsis tripteris (tall tickseed) is hands down my favorite coreopsis. It is a remarkable plant for several reasons. First, it grows up to 6 feet (1.8 m) tall. Second, it doesn't need to be staked. Third, it produces an infinite number of flowers, each one with a brown disk and yellow rays. I also love it because it blooms later in the season than other tickseeds do. I grow it with raspberry pink bee balm and tall, light blue asters. Stunning!

The foliage of *Coriandrum sativum* is known as cilantro while the seeds are called coriander. But no matter what you call it, the flowers are perfect nectar sources for the likes of syrphid flies, tachinid flies, parasitic wasps, and many other natural enemies.

The outermost flowers on each umbel have petals that project outward.

and featherlike leaves along the flowering stem. The plant itself is delicately branched and often becomes top-heavy in full flower. Staking is necessary if you expect a perfectly upright specimen. At full flower, cilantro/coriander stands 2 feet (0.6 m) high, and the flowers borne on the hairless stems are charming, loose umbels of white or pale pink flowers. Each umbel cluster is a mere 1 to 2 inches (2.5–5 cm) across and, fascinatingly, the flower petals projecting toward the outside of the umbel are longer and broader, while those pointing inward are far shorter. To me, the combination of petal sizes makes the flower look fragile and sweet.

Cilantro does best in full to partial sun and average garden soil. Because cilantro production is best in cool weather, plant seeds in early spring or fall in northern climes, and in fall or winter in the South. Once the plant begins to send up a flower stalk, stop harvesting and allow the flowers to open. Soon the plant will be buzzing with lacewings, ladybugs, syrphid flies, parasitic wasps, tachinid flies, soldier beetles, minute pirate bugs, and lots of other natural enemies and pollinators. Allowing the plant to drop seed creates a continual production cycle but does indeed limit the potential harvest of coriander.

● ●

Cosmos bipinnatus
garden cosmos, Mexican aster, common cosmos
FAMILY Asteraceae (aster)
- annual
- North American native
- blooms spring to fall
- 2–6 feet (0.6–1.8 m) high, 1–2 feet (0.3–0.6 m) wide

This native of Mexico has become a common garden plant. It is easy to grow from seed and often found as nursery-grown transplants. Cosmos has leaves with threadlike segments and a feathery appearance. Multiple varieties are available, including those with a smaller stature, bicolored petals, quilled petals, and semi-double or fully double flowers. Rays can be pink, white, red, purple, or lavender, and the central disk flowers are yellow. All prefer full to partial sun and may require staking in windy areas. Garden cosmos readily self-sows and may become weedy if not deadheaded. The flowers and foliage are an attractive source of food and habitat for tachinid flies, parasitic wasps, lacewings, syrphid flies, minute pirate bugs, spiders, ladybugs, big-eyed bugs, damsel bugs, and other beneficial insects.

Other insectary species: A similar-looking U.S. native cosmos is *Cosmos parviflorus* (syn. *Coreopsis parviflora*) or southwestern cosmos. It, too, has feathery foliage and grows to 2 to 3 feet (0.6–1 m) high. The flowers have eight lavender petals and a yellow center. Seeds of *C. parviflorus* are common in southwestern wildflower blends.

Garden cosmos (*Cosmos bipinnatus*) is an easy-to-grow annual that has feathery foliage and a tall stature, and bears a plethora of blooms.

The numerous species of native buckwheats include *Eriogonum grande* var. *rubescens*. Nearly all species are native to the western and southwestern United States and are drought resistant.

Dasiphora fruticosa **subsp.** *floribunda*

shrubby cinquefoil, bush cinquefoil, golden hardhack

SYNONYMS *Potentilla fruticosa, Dasiphora fruticosa*

FAMILY Rosaceae (rose)

- evergreen or deciduous shrub, USDA zones 2–7
- North American native
- blooms summer to fall
- 2–4 feet (0.6–1.25 m) high and as wide

Shrubby cinquefoil bears innumerable 1-inch (2.5 cm), buttercup-like flowers with five petals that appear from summer through fall. This tough plant is tolerant of varied soil conditions and thrives in full to part sun. Its leaves are divided into three to seven leaflets and appear more delicate than they actually are. In some parts of the country they remain evergreen throughout the winter; here in Pennsylvania this shrub is deciduous. Its value to predators and parasitoids is undeniable. The flowers are very enticing to many natural enemies, including ladybugs, syrphid flies, wasps, minute pirate bugs, parasitic wasps, and green lacewings. Its foliage also serves as critical shelter for assassin and damsel bugs, big-eyed bugs, spined soldier bugs, and many others.

Shrubby cinquefoil is native to a large portion of North America, including nearly all of Canada, the northern half of the United States, the Great Plains, and the entire West. I cannot say enough about its adaptability and versatility as an insectary plant and a garden specimen. If you cannot find a nursery-propagated source of the general species, one of the dozens and dozens of cultivars of shrubby cinquefoil available in the nursery trade would be a good substitute. The cultivars display far more variety in their available flower colors; selections bear pink, white, and even orange flowers in addition to the classic yellow.

Shrubby cinquefoil (*Dasiphora fruticosa* subsp. *floribunda*) is a North American native shrub that bears yellow buttercup-like flowers. Cultivars in the nursery trade also produce flowers in shades of pink, yellow, white, and orange.

....

Eriogonum species

native buckwheat, wild buckwheat, many species-specific common names

FAMILY Polygonaceae (buckwheat)

* some annuals; perennial and shrub species with varied hardiness
* North American natives
* blooms spring to fall
* sizes vary by species

The genus *Eriogonum* contains many species of plants useful for the insectary border. Nearly all of them are natives of the western and southwestern United States and do not tolerate colder climates. Some are perennials or shrubs, while others are annuals. However, most are resistant to drought; thrive in hot, arid climates; and are magnets for butterflies and natural enemies, including lacewings, ladybugs, syrphid flies, parasitic wasps, tachinid flies, big-eyed bugs, damsel bugs, and minute pirate bugs. I'll mention just a handful of the many valuable insectary species here.

Eriogonum annuum, annual native buckwheat, has a very broad native range (across the Great Plains from Texas north to Montana and everywhere in between). It is skeletal in appearance with slender leaves 2 inches (5 cm) long covered in downy hairs on unbranched stems. The flowers are creamy white and organized in loosely arranged, flat-topped clusters. Late in the season, the

St. Catherine's lace (*Eriogonum giganteum*) is one of my favorite native buckwheats—despite the fact that I cannot grow it in my northeastern garden.

flowers turn a lovely muted pink. *Eriogonum annuum* is best started from seed, though the seeds can be difficult to find for purchase. This plant may become an aggressive self-sower in certain regions.

Another excellent choice is *Eriogonum fasciculatum*, a fairly common western species known as California buckwheat. It is a shrub that reaches 4 or more feet (1.25 m) high and 3 feet (1 m) wide and produces orbs of tiny pale pink to white flowers. California buckwheat is winter hardy to 20 degrees F. Another stunning species bearing the common name St. Catherine's lace (*E. giganteum*) is smothered in foot-wide clusters of white flowers. It is by far one of my favorite native buckwheats, but unless I move west I'll probably never be able to grow it. St. Catherine's lace grows 3 feet (1 m) high and equally as wide; it, too, is hardy to 20 degrees F.

Two more species I'd like to mention are *Eriogonum corymbosum*, crispleaf buckwheat; and *E. umbellatum*, Shasta buckwheat or sulfur flower. The former is notable for its rounded masses of small white flowers and the latter for its gobs of yellow flowers and ground-hugging habit. *Eriogonum umbellatum* and its many varieties and cultivars are wonderful, insect-friendly ground covers.

Erysimum perofskianum 'Gold Shot' is at home in my USDA zone 5 Pennsylvania garden, where it provides early-season nectar for beneficial bugs.

Erysimum species

wallflower

SYNONYM *Cheiranthus*

FAMILY Brassicaceae (cabbage)

- annual, short-lived perennial, hardiness dependent on species
- some North American natives, others introduced
- blooms spring to summer
- 1–2 feet (0.3–0.6 m) high, 1 foot (0.3 m) wide, though some species are smaller and others are larger

Wallflower fills an important void in nectar availability for many beneficials, including syrphid flies, ladybugs, and lacewings. It begins to flower early in the season when other choices are limited, and many species continue to flower through the summer. Most erysimums have narrow leaves and green or gray-green foliage. Small, four-petaled flowers develop on flower stalks and open from the bottom of the stalk upward as the stem grows. Flower colors include yellow, red, cream, pink, purple, lavender, and orange.

Wallflowers prefer full sun and well-drained soils. The flowers of many species emit a sweet fragrance, especially notable in the evening. In some areas, wallflowers are treated as annuals, though many species are short-lived perennials, surviving for just a few years. They are worth the effort, though, and often self-seed.

'Bowles Mauve' wallflower (*Erysimum linifolium* 'Bowles Mauve') lines the driveway of a home in Monterey, California. I have this plant in my Pennsylvania garden, but I grow it as an annual because it doesn't always survive the winter.

Many native species of wallflower exist, including *Erysimum asperum*, the western wallflower, which bears bright yellow to orange flowers; *E. inconspicuum*, the shy wallflower, a very hardy yellow flowering native of the northern half of North America; and *E. capitatum*, the sand dune wallflower, which bears sunny orange flowers and has numerous subspecies and varieties. Many other regional natives exist as well.

Introduced species are also found across North America, with some of them having naturalized enough to obtain noxious weed status in certain regions. *Erysimum linifolium*, the purple wallflower; *E. repandum*, yellow-flowered spreading wallflower; and *E. perofskianum* are just a few nonnative species commonly found in the wild and in the nursery trade. Dozens of wallflower species, cultivars, and varieties are out there, and some are better at supporting beneficials than others. When in doubt, choose a regional native species if possible to ensure the plant's ability to support your local good bugs.

• •

Eupatorium perfoliatum

common boneset, American boneset, thoroughwort

FAMILY Asteraceae (aster)

- perennial, USDA zones 3-8
- North American native
- blooms midsummer to fall
- 3-6 feet (1-1.8 m) high, 2-4 feet (0.6-1.25 m) wide

Native to damp prairies, boneset prefers average to wet soil and is very tolerant of both low and high light levels. The clump-forming plants bear flat-topped clusters of tiny white, fuzzy flowers that are magnets for beneficial bugs, butterflies, and bees of all sorts. In Michigan State University's native plant trial, common boneset was found to host twenty times more natural enemies than control plantings of grass; in fact, it was the most attractive late-season bloomer they tested. Boneset hosts tachinid flies, parasitic wasps, minute pirate bugs, damsel bugs, ladybugs, and many other natural enemies. In my own garden, boneset is deer-resistant—an added bonus for many gardeners.

Another distinguishing feature of this plant is its leaf structure. The base of each pair of leaves is fused together and fully clasps the stem, lending the appearance of the stem passing through the leaf (hence the species name *perfoliatum*—"through the leaf"). At one time, the leaves were regularly used as a folk remedy for fevers and colds, and were thought to aid in the healing of broken bones and Dengue fever (known as breakbone fever). Common boneset is difficult to start from seed because of poor germination rates, so start plants from divisions or nursery stock if possible.

Other insectary species: Another native *Eupatorium* species, *E. serotinum* (late boneset), has similar clusters of white flowers, but its leaves do not clasp the stem. Instead they are borne on short leaf stalks (petioles).

The flowers of boneset (*Eupatorium perfoliatum*) attract a myriad of natural enemies and native pollinators.

Boneset's species name—*perfoliatum*—means "through the leaf." Here you can see how the leaves fully clasp the stem, making it appear as if the stem is passing through the leaf.

Late boneset is also known to be attractive to many natural enemies and plays host to a great diversity of parasitic wasps.

● ●

Fagopyrum esculentum
common buckwheat

FAMILY Polygonaceae (buckwheat)

- annual
- native to Eurasia
- blooms spring through fall
- 2–3 feet (0.6–1 m) high, 1–2 feet (0.3–0.6 m) wide

For many people, the name *buckwheat* conjures thoughts of pancakes and airplane pillows, but farmers have long known this plant for the benefits it provides both their soil and their good bugs. Buckwheat thrives in full to part sun and is very tolerant of lousy soils. Its heart-shaped leaves, averaging 3 inches (7.6 cm) long, are topped with clusters of small white to pale pink flowers that have what I consider a very pleasant scent, though subtle. The nectar and cover buckwheat provides are known to benefit assassin bugs, damsel bugs, spiders, syrphid flies, ladybugs, predaceous beetles, tachinid flies, parasitic wasps, minute pirate bugs, big-eyed bugs, spined soldier bugs, and others.

Field trials at Cornell University found that buckwheat strips in agricultural settings dramatically reduce the number of Colorado potato beetles that survive to adulthood in adjacent potato plantings. Researchers also note that the buckwheat insectary strips are best placed every four to six potato rows. At home, consider including a few buckwheat plants in your garden to provide an early, late, or even winter nectar source as well as habitat for your beneficials.

Common buckwheat (*Fagopyrum esculentum*) flowers just a few weeks after planting, providing a quick soil cover and feeding many different insects.

Buckwheat is grown as a spring cover crop or a frost-susceptible fall cover crop in the North. Southern farmers and gardeners can plant it in the fall for a winter cover crop.

Buckwheat is extremely fast growing. It flowers just a few weeks after planting, begins to go to seed in a mere six weeks, and has completed its life cycle in only ten to twelve weeks. Because of its rapid growth, buckwheat has become a favorite cover crop. In the North, buckwheat is grown as a spring cover crop or a frost-susceptible fall cover crop. The cover it provides prevents soil erosion, displaces weeds, and adds organic matter to the soil. Southern farmers and gardeners plant a cover of buckwheat in the winter to keep fields from becoming a fallow welcome mat for the weeds.

Because buckwheat has such a fast-paced life cycle, it's fairly easy to incorporate into crop rotation systems, though care must be taken to not allow the plants to drop seed; buckwheat can be invasive if left to self-sow. Be sure to cut the plant down, or pull it out, before the flowers have fully matured—usually about ten days after they open.

A tiny parasitic wasp feeds on the nectar of buckwheat flowers, as do many other beneficials.

Helianthus annuus

common sunflower, wild sunflower, sunflower

FAMILY Asteraceae (aster)
- annual
- North American native
- blooms summer through frost
- 1–10 feet (0.3–3 m) high, depending on variety

Sunflowers are a beautiful sight. They are bold and colorful—and so very easy to grow.

At home in nearly every garden, they require little more than full sun and average garden soil. This U.S. native has naturalized across all of North America and once served as a staple food source for Native Americans. Cultivated varieties are grown commercially for both oil and seed production, and in home gardens for their attractiveness and diversity. Sunflowers are so common that a handful of states now list them as a secondary noxious weed.

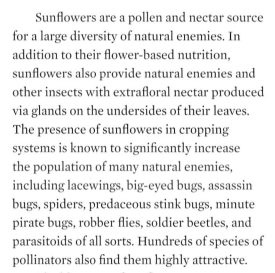

The depth of the nectaries in the central disk flowers on any given sunflower determines which insects are able to access the nectar. But the pollen on all sunflowers (except pollenless varieties) is borne on exposed anthers, making it readily accessible to many different insects.

Sunflowers are a pollen and nectar source for a large diversity of natural enemies. In addition to their flower-based nutrition, sunflowers also provide natural enemies and other insects with extrafloral nectar produced via glands on the undersides of their leaves. The presence of sunflowers in cropping systems is known to significantly increase the population of many natural enemies, including lacewings, big-eyed bugs, assassin bugs, spiders, predaceous stink bugs, minute pirate bugs, robber flies, soldier beetles, and parasitoids of all sorts. Hundreds of species of pollinators also find them highly attractive.

The blossoms of sunflowers are not a single large flower but rather a grouping of thousands of tiny individual flowers organized into a central disc shape. Careful examination shows a pattern of two opposite flower spirals in each flower head (fabulous Fibonacci!). These small disk flowers are then surrounded with one or more rows of ray flowers (petals).

Each of the tiny disk flowers requires pollination to produce a seed, and the nectary within each flower is fully concealed at the base of the style (the tube that separates the ovary from the pollen-receiving stigma).

The depth of the nectary depends on the genetics of the particular variety, making the nectar of some varieties more accessible than others—which may explain, at least in part, why certain pollinators and natural enemies visit some sunflower varieties more than others. The pollen, however, is borne on exposed anthers and is readily available to many insects—except, of course, in the case of pollenless sunflower varieties (marketed as such), which might be good for the vase but are a poor choice for the good bugs who depend on the protein present in the missing pollen. Evidence also exists that the straight species is better forage for beneficial insects and pollinators than many of the cultivated varieties.

While it's not surprising that sunflower cultivar breeders are seeking traits like increased bloom time, sturdier stems, larger seeds for oil production, increased branching, and improved flower color, it is interesting to note that some breeders are also looking to develop varieties with shallower nectaries and a higher nectar volume in hopes of increasing pollination rates and insect diversity, as well as increasing honey production.

Other insectary species: A similar species, *Helianthus petiolaris*, the prairie sunflower, is another excellent native choice. It is also an annual and is smaller in stature, though it prefers sandier soils.

● ●

Heliopsis helianthoides

smooth oxeye, oxeye sunflower, false sunflower

FAMILY Asteraceae (aster)

Smooth oxeye 'Summer Sun' (*Heliopsis helianthoides* 'Summer Sun') is not just a beautiful addition to the garden. It is also capable of supporting many natural enemies, as well as the prey insects they rely on.

- perennial, USDA zones 3–9
- North American native
- blooms mid to late summer
- 3–5 feet (1–1.5 m) high, 2–4 feet (0.6–1.25 m) wide

At a Master Gardener conference where I once spoke, we had the opportunity to visit a nearby botanic garden that included a pollinator garden, filled with plants perfectly suited to foraging pollinators. Heliopsis was one of the featured plants. As I was walking through the garden with several of the Master Gardeners, we noticed the heliopsis stems were loaded with thousands of deep red aphids. One of the women said, "I wonder why they haven't taken care of those." And I, of course, couldn't keep my mouth shut and began to explain about all the natural enemies that were probably already there

'Tuscan Sun' heliopsis (*Heliopsis helianthoides* 'Tuscan Sun') has a smaller stature and rich orange-yellow flowers.

Heliopsis has serrated leaves that are rounded at the base and taper to a point. Both the ray flowers and central disk flowers are yellow-orange. The plant is clump forming and drought tolerant and, if deadheaded, has a long season of bloom. The many available cultivars include 'Prairie Sunset', with an orange band on the petals; 'Ballerina', a semi-double form; and 'Summer Sun', my own standby variety. Heliopsis is indeed prone to aphid attacks, which now you know isn't necessarily a bad thing. The plants are quite tolerant of the aphids and could even be used as nursery plants to provide natural enemies with a free aphid lunch and encourage them to stick around and manage the real problems.

● ●

Leucanthemum ×*superbum*
Shasta daisy

FAMILY Asteraceae (aster)
- perennial, USDA zones 5–9
- native to Europe
- blooms mid to late summer
- 1–4 feet (0.3–1.25 m) high, 3–4 feet (1–1.25 m) wide

Shastas are classic-looking daisies—a central core of tiny yellow disk flowers surrounded by white ray flowers. Each of these inflorescences measures 2 or more inches (5 cm) across. The plant's glossy dark green leaves have small teeth on their margins and create good habitat for predatory bugs like assassin, damsel, and

taking care of the aphid situation and how spraying would harm them as well. We began to look at the plants very carefully and within moments had spotted numerous beneficials, including spined soldier bug eggs, three species of ladybugs, green lacewing eggs and an adult, a brown lacewing larva, multiple parasitized aphid mummies, several adult parasitic wasps, tachinid flies, syrphid flies, and even a syrphid fly pupa. It was very eye opening to the group, and they continued to look through the plants for more signs of natural enemies until we had to get back to the conference.

spined soldier bugs. The nectar and pollen from the flowers is preferred by some species of parasitic wasps, minute pirate bugs, lacewings, soldier beetles, ladybugs, and syrphid flies.

I propose that you plant this daisy instead of the oxeye daisy (*Chrysanthemum leucanthemum*, syn. *Leucanthemum vulgare*), which is often recommended for insectary plantings but is also on the noxious weed list for many states. Oxeye daisy does, indeed, support beneficials, but it is an aggressive grower that overtakes pastures and displaces native plant species. Although the Shasta daisy, too, is a European introduction, it is far less assertive and is also an attractive garden plant and cut flower.

The dozens of cultivars of this plant range in size from barely 1 foot (0.3 m) to more than 4 feet (1.25 m) tall. Taller varieties may require staking if they aren't positioned in a preferred sunny site. 'Becky' reaches 3 to 4 feet (1–1.25 m) tall and produces its main flush of blooms in June and then a smattering

'Becky' is a Shasta cultivar that produces blooms for many weeks on sturdy dark green plants. I grow it in my garden, where this photo was taken.

of blooms a few weeks after it is deadheaded. Many Shasta cultivars offer double or semi-double flowers with multiple rows of petals. They have tempted me on occasion, but evidence exists that the nectar and pollen from these double flowers are harder for natural enemies to access. So for now, I'll let 'Becky' shine in my garden.

● ●

Levisticum officinale
lovage, garden lovage

SYNONYMS *Hipposelinum levisticum, Levisticum paludapifolium*

FAMILY Apiaceae (carrot)

- perennial, USDA zones 3–8
- native to the Mediterranean region
- blooms late spring to early summer
- 3–7 feet (1–2 m) high, 3–5 feet (1–1.5 m) wide

My mother grew lovage in her garden when I was a kid, yet I never once saw her use it in

The flowers of Shasta daisies (*Leucanthemum* ×*superbum*) provide shelter, pollen, and nectar to natural enemies, including this ladybug larva.

Lovage (*Levisticum officinale*) tops out at an amazing 7 feet (2 m) or more. The flower heads are made of many tiny yellow-green flowers, and the entire plant is edible.

edible greens, stalks, roots, and seeds and use it to flavor everything from soups and stews to sweets, but I let the syrphid flies, parasitic wasps, ladybugs, lacewings, and tachinid flies use it for their dinner.

The flower heads of lovage each comprise an enormous number of very tiny yellow-green flowers. Arranged together, they can reach up to 8 inches (20 cm) across, and the hollow flowering stems can top out at 7 feet (2 m) or more. The leaves of lovage look a bit like celery on steroids. They comprise numerous leaflets that get smaller as they progress higher up the flowering stalk. It's an imposing plant that prefers full sun and average garden soil. Give it a lot of space.

In southern climes, lovage will not survive. It needs a winter dormancy and doesn't do well in continual heat, but lovage has naturalized across much of the Northeast and parts of the West. It readily self-sows, and its thick, fleshy taproot expands fairly quickly to form a sizeable clump. I suggest you deadhead the plant before the seeds ripen and burst open.

If you are looking for something similar but with a far smaller stature, consider growing parsley (*Petroselinum crispum*). Because it is a biennial that forms only a rosette of leaves the first season, you'll need to allow it to overwinter and come into flower early the following year. Parsley's flowers are also attractive to many natural enemies.

the kitchen. I always marveled at the enormity of the plant and enjoyed breaking off the leaves and inhaling the celery-like scent, but because it never became a kitchen favorite, the plant wasn't long for our garden and was eventually removed. Now I realize the value of this plant to all the beneficials flitting around my garden and know its worth lies not just in its good looks and fresh scent. Once I was served a delicious Bloody Mary that had a section of hollow lovage stem used as a natural straw. Others enjoy this plant for its

Low-growing sweet alyssum (*Lobularia maritima*) is smothered in tiny flowers. It readily self sows and is grown as an annual in most areas, except for the extreme South where it is a perennial.

Sweet alyssum's seeds require light to germinate. Flowers can be white, pink, purple, peach, or lavender.

● ●

Lobularia maritima
sweet alyssum

SYNONYMS *Alyssum odoratum, Cylpeola maritima, Koniga maritima*

FAMILY Brassicaceae (cabbage)

- perennial in USDA zones 10–11; grown as an annual elsewhere
- native to southern Europe
- blooms spring through frost
- 3–8 inches (7.6–20 cm) high, 1 foot (0.3 m) wide

This plant may be small, but it is enticing to many natural enemies in a big way. Sweet alyssum is most often grown as an annual, and its short stature makes it a great choice for the front of the insectary border, in between crop rows, or in containers. It is frequently grown as a companion plant on organic lettuce farms because of its ability to attract a large number of beneficials, including parasitic wasps, tachinid flies, lacewings, big-eyed bugs, hoverflies, and many others. Cabbage growers also find it useful for increasing the lifespan of the parasitic wasps that control many common cabbage pests.

Sweet alyssum bears scores of tiny, four-petaled flowers that measure a mere 1/4 inch across. The flowers occur in globular clusters on branched stems and can be white, pink, peach, purple, or lavender. They are honey scented and grow best in full to part sun. The plants are also fairly tolerant of dry soil, though flowering slows in hot weather. Sweet alyssum is easily grown from surface-sown seeds (the seeds need light to germinate), and transplants are a common find at garden centers in the spring. Because of its tendency to self-sow, sweet alyssum has become naturalized across much of the United States and is recognized in California as potentially invasive.

Each year I plant sweet alyssum at the top of my rock retaining wall as I enjoy it cascading over the wall's edge. I especially like the frothy white blooms in the evening when their color reflects the fading light and their fragrance is the sweetest. Sweet alyssum also finds a home each year beneath my roses. It is attractive to several species of parasitic wasps that always keep my rose-sucking aphid populations in check.

The short, tubular flowers of horsemint (*Monarda punctata*) are arranged in whorls around the stem and readily accessed by smaller bugs.

● ●

Monarda punctata
horsemint, spotted bee balm, spotted horsemint

FAMILY Lamiaceae (mint)

- perennial, USDA zones 4–9
- North American native
- blooms summer through early fall
- 1.5–3 feet (0.5–1 m) high, 2–4 feet (0.6–1.25 m) wide or more

Horsemint garners a lot of attention in the garden. Like other members of the genus *Monarda*, it has hollow, square stems; but unlike many other monardas, horsemint bears short, tubular yellowish flowers with purple spots. Nectar from these flowers is more readily accessed by smaller bugs, while monardas

Native to North America, horsemint is particularly attractive to beneficials late in the season.

with more elongated flowers are often preferred by butterflies, bees, and moths. Native plant research at Michigan State University found horsemint to be attractive to a large diversity of natural enemies, particularly late in the season. Not only does horsemint attract a plethora of good bugs, but it is also drought defiant, deer resistant, powdery mildew tolerant, and incredibly visually interesting.

Oregano (*Origanum vulgare*) has numerous subspecies and cultivars, nearly all of which support beneficial insects.

The small flowers of horsemint are arranged in clusters around the flowering stem. Beneath each cluster of flowers is a whorl of showy pink to purple bracts. The flower whorls occur in tiers down the stem with a section of bare stem separating each flower cluster. The leaves of horsemint are fragrant and were—and still are—used to make a tea to treat all sorts of bodily ailments.

Horsemint is a native of the eastern and southern United States, parts of the southwestern United States and California, as well as parts of Canada and is listed as endangered in several regions. It self-sows quite readily and can be started from cuttings, root divisions, and fall-planted seeds. With the exception of full shade, it thrives in nearly every garden setting.

● ●

Origanum vulgare
oregano, European oregano, wild marjoram
FAMILY Lamiaceae (mint)
- perennial in USDA zones 5–9, though some varieties are hardier than others
- native to the Mediterranean region
- blooms mid to late summer
- 1–2 feet (0.3–0.6 m) high, 2 feet (0.6 m) wide

Most oregano varieties produce clusters of tiny white, pink, or purple flowers atop stems lined with medium-sized oval leaves. Though oregano is considered a culinary herb, its benefits to the insectary border are as obvious as can be. Not only is oregano useful to beneficials for its nectar, pollen, and user-friendly flower shape, but it also has the ideal habit for many ground-dwelling beneficials. On a summer afternoon, I love to sit near oregano and just watch it buzz with life. If I get close enough, I can spot some pretty interesting critters. On the oregano in the dead center of my vegetable garden, I regularly find minute pirate bugs, parasitic wasps, hoverflies, tachinid flies, soldier beetles, lacewing larva, and big-eyed bugs. There are always plenty of bees and butterflies, too. And if I lift up the plant's skirt and check out the soil beneath, I'm likely to find a handful of spiders and ground beetles scurrying about as well.

The specimen in my vegetable garden is *Origanum vulgare* var. *hirtum*, commonly known as Greek or Italian oregano, one of many subspecies and cultivars of this perennial herb. Each different selection has a slightly different flavor; my particular variety is used in my kitchen to flavor pizza, pasta, salad dressings, and lots of other dishes. Nearly all the subspecies and varieties of this herb are helpful to your good bugs, so even if your palate differs from mine, there are plenty of choices. It's possible to reap both the culinary and the insectary benefits by harvesting what you want for the kitchen while the plant is young, and then allowing the plant to come into flower to benefit your good bugs.

Other insectary species: *Origanum majorana* (synonyms *Majorana hortensis*, *M. majorana*), commonly known as sweet marjoram, is another useful option, though it has limited hardiness and is grown as a perennial only in USDA zones 8 and above; elsewhere it's grown as an annual. It too bears small white to lavender flowers that provide for certain beneficials.

● ●

Phacelia tanacetifolia
lacy phacelia, fiddleneck
FAMILY Hydrophyllaceae (waterleaf)
- annual
- North American native
- blooms summer through fall
- 1–2 feet (0.3–0.6 m) high, 1 foot (0.3 m) wide

The common name fiddleneck says it all when

The sweet marjoram (*Origanum majorana*) I grow as an annual in my garden hosts a green lacewing larva.

Lacy phacelia (*Phacelia tanacetifolia*) is often used as a cover crop and bee forage. This adaptable and fascinating plant is a North American native.

All members of the genus *Phacelia* have coiled flowers and elongated stamens. And all serve to support a diversity of pollinators and natural enemies.

it comes to the flowers of this native of the Southwest. Small purple-blue blossoms unfurl from a coiled flower stalk (Fibonacci and his sequence strike again!) that produces blooms over a very long period of time. The amazing organization of this flower enthralls me every time I see it. The elongated stamens within each flower extend out, making the uncurling flowers look whiskered and fuzzy. With its captivating flowers and lacelike foliage, lacy phacelia is a great plant for supporting syrphid flies, tachinid flies, certain parasitic wasps, and the many predatory true bugs that use it as cover.

Often sold as a green manure, bee forage, and cover crop, lacy phacelia is a very adaptable plant, tolerant of different climates and soil types. It does prefer full sun, but lacy phacelia can also be grown in partial shade. It blooms a mere six to eight weeks after germinating. Because it germinates and grows so rapidly, it is a popular cover crop in Europe and is somewhat popular in vineyards and farms in western North America as a fall/winter field cover, though it does not survive winter temperatures below 20 degrees F. In many cases the plant self-sows, creating a nice colony that continues year to year. Be warned that the stems of this plant are covered in small hairs that can irritate skin.

Other insectary species: A close relative, *Phacelia integrifolia*, is another frequently recommended insectary plant because of its ability to support many bee species, both native and introduced.

● ●

Pimpinella anisum
anise, aniseed, saxifrage
SYNONYM *Anisum vulgare*
FAMILY Apiaceae (carrot)
- annual
- native to the Mediterranean region
- blooms midsummer
- 1–3 feet (0.3–1.25 m) high, 1 foot (0.3 m) wide

Not only is anise a great nectar and pollen source for natural enemies, it is also an

Anise (*Pimpinella anisum*) is readily grown from seed and is a great nectar and pollen source for beneficials. Its edible foliage lends a licorice flavor in the kitchen.

Pycnanthemum muticum (short-toothed, clustered, or big leaf mountain mint) is a favorite in my garden and is constantly swarmed with pollinators and beneficials of all sorts.

attractive addition to any garden—and to the kitchen. The leaves and seeds of this herb lend a licorice flavor to both savory and sweet dishes (Italian anise-flavored pizzelles are a personal favorite). Most commonly grown from seed, anise produces umbrella-shaped clusters of tiny white flowers known to support many species of parasitic wasps, ladybugs, lacewings, tachinid flies, and other beneficial insects. The bright green leaves at the base of the plant are broad and gently lobed but farther up the stem are finely feathered, lending the plant a soft, graceful feel.

Pycnanthemum **species**

mountain mint

FAMILY Lamiaceae (mint)

- perennial, USDA zones 3–9, depending on species
- North American native
- blooms in summer
- 2–4 feet (0.6–1.25 m) high, 2–3 feet (0.6–1 m) wide

About twenty species of mountain mint are native to North America, and several of them are threatened or endangered in one or more states. All but one species are native east of

Virginia mountain mint (*Pycnanthemum virginianum*) is one of twenty North American native species and is a magnet for good bugs.

the Rocky Mountains, with *Pycnanthemum californicum* (Sierra mint) being the only native of the West. Within the genus are several species that I see as particularly valuable garden plants. *Pycnanthemum virginianum* (Virginia mountain mint) and *P. tenuifolium* (little-leaved or slender mountain mint) look fairly similar, with small awl-shaped leaves topped with clusters of white flowers with small purple specks. They are both magnets for good bugs, luring in natural enemies and pollinators of all sorts.

But my favorite of the mountain mints is *Pycnanthemum muticum* (short-toothed, clustered, or big leaf mountain mint). The leaves of this plant are an inch (2.5 cm) or so across; surrounding each cluster of pinkish white flowers are showy silvery bracts. Visitors to my garden ask about this plant more than any

other. Every summer it is swarming with bees, butterflies, parasitic wasps, and beetles and flies of all sorts. At night I often find lacewings and moths drinking from its flowers.

All mountain mints thrive in full to partial sun and average to moist soils. They are notably deer and critter resistant, probably because of their highly fragrant foliage. Another important note about this plant: don't be turned off by the word *mint*. Mountain mint does not spread aggressively via underground stolons like members of the genus *Mentha*. Much like bee balm, it forms a dense stand. That being said, of all the *Pycnanthemum* species, *P. muticum* has the greatest tendency to get a little out of hand. It is easy to control, though, by frequently separating the clump with a shovel.

● ●

Ratibida pinnata
pinnate prairie coneflower, yellow coneflower, gray-headed prairie coneflower, drooping coneflower

SYNONYMS *Lepachys pinnata, Rudbeckia pinnata*
FAMILY Asteraceae (aster)

- perennial, USDA zones 3–9
- North American native
- blooms early to late summer
- 3–4 feet (1–1.25 m) high, 1–2 feet (0.3–0.6 m) wide

The drooping yellow petals of this plant readily distinguish it from other species. To me

The yellow coneflower (*Ratibida pinnata*) is a native perennial that prefers lean soils and requires very little care. It provides habitat and food for a variety of beneficials.

It provides both habitat and food for the likes of parasitic wasps, soldier beetles, ladybugs, tachinid flies, minute pirate bugs, spiders, syrphid flies, damsel bugs, and lacewings.

The leaves of yellow coneflower are compound with multiple segments per leaf. The elongated flower head starts out a grayish green and matures to a deep brown, and if you crush it, the cone smells of licorice. Yellow coneflower is very easy to start from seeds or transplants.

their downward curve always makes them look thirsty, but to the contrary, yellow coneflower survives just fine in soils of average moisture and requires little extra care. It is a plant that prefers lean soils, as rich, fertile soil makes its stems floppy. This native of eastern North America and the Great Plains is an exemplary plant for natural enemies.

Rudbeckia species

black-eyed Susan, many species-specific common names

FAMILY Asteraceae (aster)

- annual, biennial, or perennial in USDA zones 3–9, depending on species
- North American natives
- blooms summer through fall
- 1–10 feet (0.3–3 m) high, depending on species

Rudbeckias are some of the most robust and attractive plants around. They are no-fuss plants that require little more than average soil and full sun. The pollen and nectar of these plants support syrphid flies, tachinid flies, soldier beetles, and certain parasitic wasps. North America hosts many native species of rudbeckia, with a large number of them being region-specific. I highlight four species here for their broad geographical range and availability within the nursery trade.

Annual black-eyed Susans (*Rudbeckia hirta*) are a staple of my summer garden. Their pollen and nectar attract syrphid flies, tachinid flies, soldier beetles, and certain parasitic wasps.

This green-headed coneflower, *Rudbeckia laciniata* 'Herbstsonne', grows to an astonishing height.

Rudbeckia laciniata, the tall coneflower, cut leaf coneflower, or green-headed coneflower, is one of the tallest rudbeckias. Topping out between 3 and 12 feet (1 and 3.6 m) tall, cut leaf coneflower has divided leaves and 4-inch (10 cm) flowers that have cone-shaped green centers and downward-curved yellow rays. It is native to nearly all of North America.

Rudbeckia fulgida, the orange coneflower or black-eyed Susan, is a broad-ranging eastern native that has become a ubiquitous garden species. It has many varieties and cultivars. The yellow-orange petals and dark central disks are produced on plants reaching 1 to 3 feet (0.3 to 1 m) tall. The leaves have fine, bristly hairs.

Rudbeckia hirta, annual black-eyed Susans, are often treated as annuals or biennials in the landscape. They reach 1 to 2 feet (0.3–0.6 m) tall and have very hairy leaves and coarse stems. Many varieties and cultivars of this species exist, some bearing yellow rays and others sporting various combinations of burgundy, orange, brown, and yellow. There are double-petaled forms as well.

Rudbeckia triloba, brown-eyed Susans or thin-leaved coneflowers, are an eastern and southern species. The basal leaves of this plant are often trifoliate (meaning they comprise three leaflets joined together). The plants are multibranched and reach 2 to 3 feet (0.6 to 1 m) high, lending the plant a dense, bushy appearance. It is distinguished from *R. fulgida*

Brown-eyed Susans (*Rudbeckia triloba*) are multibranched and smothered in inch-wide flowers.

by its shorter petals, smaller flowers, and heavier branching. It is a short-lived perennial in most areas.

● ●

Silphium perfoliatum
cup plant, cup rosinweed, compass plant, Indian-cup

FAMILY Asteraceae (aster)

- perennial, USDA zones 3–9
- North American native
- blooms midsummer through fall
- 4–10 feet (1.25–3 m) high, 1–3 feet (0.3–1 m) wide

Cup plant (*Silphium perfoliatum*) is an imposing garden specimen that requires lots of room. The bright yellow flowers attract an array of beneficials.

Cup plant is one imposing garden specimen. It spreads by shallow rhizomes and can take over smaller gardens, so be sure you have plenty of room for it and are prepared to manage its growth. This native of eastern North America and the Great Plains produces tall, thick, square stems that are straight as an arrow until the flower heads branch out at the top; they exude a gooey sap when cut. The 8-inch (20 cm) leaves are opposite each other, and each leaf pair is fused together around the stem to form a cup that readily catches rainwater and is a favorite drinking spot for many different birds, butterflies, and even frogs. The flowers measure 3 inches (7.6 cm) across and have bright yellow rays and darker yellow disk flowers. The flowers serve to attract soldier bugs, minute pirate bugs, ladybugs, lacewings, spiders, and other beneficials.

• •

Solidago species
goldenrod

FAMILY Asteraceae (aster)

- perennial, USDA zones 4–9; hardiness depends on species
- North American natives
- blooms late summer through fall
- 1–4 feet (0.3–1.25 m) high, depending on species

Goldenrod was once undeservedly shunned from gardens. It was (and sadly still is) considered a weed in much of North America,

and it is often blamed for causing hay fever, though its pollen is too heavy to be carried on the wind (ragweed is the true culprit). There are more than seventy-five species of goldenrod, and many of those species have numerous varieties and cultivars. Almost all goldenrods bear golden yellow flowers on slender stems in late summer. Goldenrod's many tiny flowers are organized into inflorescences that range in appearance from spikelike clusters to plumes, balls, and even fireworks bursts, depending on the species, variety, or cultivar. Goldenrods provide pollen, nectar, and much needed habitat to soldier beetles, big-eyed bugs, minute pirate bugs, ladybugs, parasitic wasps, syrphid flies, damsel bugs, spiders, assassin bugs, and many other natural enemies.

All goldenrods prefer full sun and average to moist garden soil. Some do have a tendency to spread aggressively via their underground rhizomes. In other parts of the world where goldenrod was introduced as a garden specimen, the plant has escaped and displaced native plants and caused a problem. Though many selections exist to pick from, here I describe three species with a broad native range, an easy nature, and appeal as an insectary plant.

Solidago canadensis, or Canada goldenrod, has been found to support more than sixteen different species of parasitic wasps. It is native to nearly all of North America with the exception of the extreme Southeast and has a

Goldenrod (*Solidago*) species support numerous beneficials with their pollen and nectar, and they also host a diversity of prey insects.

Missouri goldenrod (*Solidago missouriensis*) is native west of the Mississippi River and is one of the earliest goldenrods to flower.

Solidago canadensis, Canada goldenrod, is native to nearly all of North America.

loosely arranged inflorescence shaped like an inverted cone. It reaches 2 to 4 feet (0.6 to 1.25 m) high and spreads fairly quickly. It can be distinguished from other common goldenrods by the small hairs on its foliage and stems.

Solidago altissima, tall goldenrod, late goldenrod, or Canada goldenrod, is indigenous to everywhere but the Pacific Northwest and a few other states. Its flowers occur as loose, featherlike plumes. The plant reaches 3 to 4 feet (1–1.25 m) high.

Solidago missouriensis, Missouri goldenrod, produces a dense plume of bright yellow flowers and is native west of the Mississippi River. It reaches 1 to 3 feet (0.3–1 m) high. Missouri goldenrod's stem may be pink, green, or even dark red, and both the stems and leaves are hairless. It is one of the earliest goldenrods to bloom.

• •

Spiraea alba
meadowsweet, white meadowsweet, narrowleaf meadowsweet

FAMILY Rosaceae (rose)
- deciduous shrub, USDA zones 3–7
- North American native
- blooms midsummer through fall
- 2–4 feet (0.6–1.25 m) high and as wide

This remarkable shrub deserves to be used far more than it is. Not only does it produce fragrant conical clusters of fuzzy white flowers on the tops of its upright branches, but

it thrives with little care in a wide range of growing conditions and provides nectar, pollen, and habitat for a plethora of good bugs. In trials at Michigan State University, meadowsweet was found to be one of the most attractive midseason bloomers to both beneficials and pollinators. It provides habitat and food for minute pirate bugs, parasitic wasps, assassin bugs, ladybugs, ground beetles, damsel bugs, and lots of other natural enemies.

Meadowsweet is a native of the northeastern United States across to the Dakotas

Meadowsweet (*Spiraea alba*) is a lovely yet underused shrub. Its conical white flowers borne atop upright deciduous stems are highly attractive to both beneficials and pollinators.

Spiraea tomentosa, steeplebush, is a pink-flowering, upright shrub native to eastern North America and the Pacific Northwest.

and north into Canada and grows in full to partial sun and average to wet soils. Its habit is fairly upright and narrow, even when mature, a quality I find very attractive in the insectary border. It's a shame that this lovely plant is endangered in several states when it has the potential to be a valuable and attractive landscape specimen.

Other insectary species: *Spiraea tomentosa* (steeplebush) is a pink-flowering species with very similar traits. A native of western North America, *Spiraea douglasii* (commonly known as rose spirea, western spirea, Douglas spirea, or hardhack steeplebush) is perhaps a better selection for the West than *S. alba* or *S. tomentosa*. It also bears conical clusters of flowers in a jovial pink. It's hardy in USDA zones 5–8.

● ●

Symphyotrichum species
aster, hardy aster, Michaelmas daisy

FAMILY Asteraceae (aster)

- perennial, USDA zones 3–8, depending on species
- North American natives
- blooms late summer to fall
- 1–4 feet (0.3–1.25 m) high and as wide, depending on species

Many North American native asters that used to be in the genus *Aster* are now in the genus *Symphyotrichum*; the genus *Aster* now comprises only Old World species of this plant.

New England aster (*Symphyotrichum novae-angliae*) is native to most of North America and includes numerous cultivars, including 'Purple Dome'. Asters are ultra-appealing to beneficials.

Smooth blue aster (*Symphyotrichum laeve*) is a favorite in my garden where it flowers late into the autumn.

Regardless of the nomenclature change (and the spelling and pronunciation problems we face because of it), native asters are one exceptional group of plants. Not only are they a good-looking, late-blooming, and easy-natured group, they lay out the welcome mat for natural enemies of all shapes and sizes. These plants support oodles of minute pirate bugs, parasitic wasps, damsel bugs, ladybugs, tachinid flies, and soldier beetles.

Asters are ultra-appealing to beneficials because of their late bloom time and their accessible flower structure. The blooms provide nectar and pollen very late in the season when few other plants are still going strong. The latest-flowering aster I grow is *Symphyotrichum laeve*, smooth blue aster. It easily reaches 4 feet (1.25 m) tall and is often in flower on Halloween in my USDA zone 6 garden. I love the periwinkle blue petals and sunny yellow centers.

Some ninety species of asters are native to North America, and multiple species grow in every state of the union and in every Canadian province. There are hundreds of cultivars, varieties, and subspecies of these asters. It's dizzying. Though all native asters probably support beneficials, the species I find to be noted most often as beneficial friendly are *Symphyotrichum pilosum* (hairy white oldfield aster), a native east of the Rockies; *S. novae-angliae* (New England aster), native to most of North America; and *S. ericoides* (white heath aster), native to nearly all of North America. I think whichever native aster strikes your fancy is the one to choose.

This damsel bug nymph is just one of the many natural enemies I find regularly on my feverfew plants.

• •

Tanacetum parthenium
feverfew

SYNONYMS *Chrysanthemum parthenium, Matricaria parthenium, Pyrethrum parthenium*

FAMILY Asteraceae (aster)

- perennial in USDA zones 5–9; grown as an annual below zone 5
- native of Eurasia
- blooms late spring to early summer
- 1–2 feet (0.3–0.6 m) high and as wide

Feverfew is tough as nails. Thriving in lousy soils and full to partial sun, feverfew grows like a weed, and thus the caution I give in the next paragraph. Each small daisylike inflorescence comprises hundreds of tiny yellow disk flowers surrounded by a row of white rays. The ferny foliage is heavily fragranced (I don't like the scent, but others do) and medium green. On any given day in my garden, the flowers of feverfew are crawling with tachinid flies, lacewing larvae, ladybug larvae, minute pirate bugs, syrphid flies, damsel bugs, assassin bugs, spiders, and lots of other natural enemies.

Feverfew (*Tanacetum parthenium*) aggressively self-sows—but its small flowers also support a broad range of beneficials and pollinators.

That said, be aware that this plant likes to make babies—a whole lot of babies. So much so that my stand of feverfew starts every year as a carpet of fuzzy green seedlings. I have to pull the vast majority of them out so that my other plants have room to grow. If you plan to incorporate feverfew into your own garden, be prepared to religiously deadhead it before it goes to seed. Even then you'll find yourself yanking some out.

● ●

Verbena stricta

hoary vervain, hoary verbena, tall vervain, woolly verbena, vervain

FAMILY Verbenaceae (verbena)

- short-lived perennial/annual, USDA zones 3–7
- North American native
- blooms mid to late summer
- 2–4 feet (0.6–1.25 m) high, 1 foot (0.3 m) wide

The first time I saw vervain, it was growing in a field on the organic farm my husband and I used to own. It stood alone among lots of grasses, goldenrod, and asters. Sadly, it only bloomed one year and then never returned. I now know that hoary vervain is a short-lived perennial and often survives for only a few years, requiring the seed it distributes to produce future generations. A native of most of the United States and eastern Canada, hoary vervain blooms for six weeks, performs just fine in poor soils, and is easy to start from

Hoary vervain (*Verbena stricta*) is a short-lived perennial. It is a mid-to-late-season bloomer native to most of North America.

Blue vervain (*Verbena hastata*) appears very similar to its cousin, hoary vervain, but prefers wet soils. Both are easy to start from seed.

The flowers of Culver's root (*Veronicastrum virginicum*) are attractive to native bee species, parasitic wasps, pollen-seeking syrphid flies, and minute pirate bugs.

seed. It is very drought tolerant and brings in the likes of minute pirate bugs, parasitic wasps, damsel bugs, spiders, and lacewings.

Hoary vervain's pink to purple flowers are produced on branched spikes atop narrow, unbranched stems. The individual quarter-inch (0.6 cm) blossoms appear in a ring around the flowering stem and then proceed to open, one or two rings at a time, from the bottom of the spike upward. The leaves are oval with serrated edges and are covered in fine white hairs—especially on their undersides—giving the plant a muted gray color. The gray foliage and purple flowers look very striking against a green backdrop. It is a plant that provides the greatest visual impact from not just a single specimen but a whole bunch of them growing en masse. Imagine my excitement all those years ago if I had spotted a throng of them rather than just a lone stalk.

Other insectary species: Blue vervain (*Verbena hastata*) looks and acts very similar to hoary vervain but prefers damper soils. It, too, is welcoming to good bugs and bees of all sorts.

● ● ● ● ● ● ● ● ● ● ● ● ● ● ● ● ● ● ● ●

Veronicastrum virginicum
Culver's root, Bowman's root
SYNONYM *Leptandra virginica, Veronica virginica*
FAMILY Scrophulariaceae (figwort)
- perennial, USDA zones 3–8
- North American native

- blooms mid to late summer
- 3–6 feet (1–1.8 m) high, 2–4 feet (0.6–1.25 m) wide

Culver's root is a striking plant. It produces 6-foot (1.8 m) candelabras of flowering stems. Each stem consists of many small white flowers clustered together and opening from bottom to top. The elongated stamens lend a fuzzy appearance to each flower, making the stem's collection of flowers look like a narrow bottlebrush. The long, serrated leaves of Culver's root are arranged in distinctive whorls around the stem. This is a particularly good plant for many native bee species and is also attractive to parasitic wasps, pollen-seeking syrphid flies, and minute pirate bugs. Other natural enemies use it for shelter and egg-laying sites.

Preferring full sun to partial shade and average to wet soil, Culver's root is native to all of North America east of the Rockies. If it's grown in less than full sun, plan to stake it for support. New plants can be started readily via crown divisions or stem cuttings.

• •

Zizia aurea

golden zizia, golden alexanders

FAMILY Apiaceae (carrot)

- perennial, USDA zones 4–9
- North American native
- blooms late spring to early summer
- 1–3 feet (0.3–1 m) high, 2 feet (0.6 m) wide

Golden zizia (*Zizia aurea*) is among the first plants to flower in my insectary border. Its sunny yellow umbels reach several inches across.

Heartleaf golden alexanders (*Zizia aptera*) is another beautiful, early-blooming choice for the insectary garden.

The zizia in my garden regularly hosts natural enemies like this assassin bug nymph, syrphid flies, parasitic wasps, and many others.

Golden zizia arrived in my garden via my native-plant-loving friend Diane. She gave me a large chunk of it in a plastic grocery bag about eight years ago. I was completely unfamiliar with the plant at the time, but it has since become one of my favorite native perennials. *Zizia aurea* is a magnet for good bugs, including many predators and parasitoids, as well as bees and butterflies. It is an exceptional early season nectar source for many species. Each spring my zizia is buzzing with dozens of parasitic wasps so small they are barely noticeable—except, of course, to someone who knows to look for them.

It's also a very attractive plant, with brilliant yellow, Queen Anne's lace–like flowers. Each inflorescence is a cluster of scores of tiny flowers that together create a compound umbel up to 4 inches (10 cm) across. Though zizia's bloom time is fairly short, about three weeks, the subsequent seedpods are also attractive, as is the medium green foliage—which tinges a deep plum color in the autumn. The leaves look much like those of celery, with serrated edges and a compound, lobed leaf structure.

Because I knew nothing about this plant upon its arrival, I positioned it completely inappropriately. Golden zizia prefers wet soils and full sun. Instead I planted it in the dry shade beneath a maple tree in my front yard. Thankfully, it is an incredibly forgiving plant and has not only survived but thrived. Zizia is notably deer resistant, self-seeds quite nicely,

and has excellent natural, and forced, germination rates. What started as a colony of one in my garden is now several dozen strong with enough seedlings left as hand-me-downs for other gardening friends. After the seeds have dropped, you can remove the dead flower stalks to tidy the plant. In late summer, the foliage can flop and yellow; simply cut out any less-than-perfect leaves and fresh new ones will grow.

Other insectary species: A sister species, heartleaf golden alexanders (*Zizia aptera*), is another excellent choice for the insectary border. It, too, is highly attractive to beneficials, blooms in the spring, and bears yellow umbrella-shaped flower clusters. It is native to most of North America except for the southwestern United States and New England, and tolerates drier soils than *Z. aurea*. It is easily distinguished from *Z. aurea* by its foliage. The basal leaves are elongated with a serrated edge and get smaller higher up the plant. The leaves closest to the flowers become compound and have three to four lobes.

your
beneficial
border

a guide to designing
for the bugs

Designing an insectary border that is appealing to both beneficial insects and humans isn't as difficult as it might seem. The challenge is to include a diversity of flower shapes, plan for continuous in-season bloom, create year-round habitat, and blend plants together in an appealing manner, as this garden has done.

a s you already know, many natural enemies feed not only on other insects but also on nectar and pollen. Insectary plantings, or insectary borders, are areas intentionally created to support the nutritional and environmental needs of insect predators and parasitoids. These areas can come about simply by letting part of the yard or farm go wild, but often they are purposefully created. They are designed and maintained specifically to cater to the needs of beneficial insects.

The design of the border greatly influences the types of predators and parasitoids

lured to it, as well as the length of their stay and even their health and well-being. Several factors are involved in such consequences, including the diversity of flower shapes and bloom times, the complexity of plant architectures, and the creation of winter habitat. Blending all these factors together with some sense of aesthetic appeal can prove challenging. This chapter shows you how to do it.

Here you will learn how to use all the plants profiled in the previous chapter, and some others as well, to develop a diverse environment that encourages beneficial insects of all sorts. Just so you won't be intimidated by the design process, I provide a handful of insectary border plans for you to use as a guide. You can take the ideas presented here and adapt them to your own landscape based on your aesthetic sense, your gardening climate, and the size of your backyard.

biocontrol tactics for your yard

I once had a discussion with an insect-loathing friend (yes, I do have a few of those) about our food future. After I mentioned the decline in European honeybee numbers and its effect on crop production, she said, "Well, I guess we just won't have any more honey." I then began a gentle rant about how the missing honey will be the least of our problems if we don't work on preserving pollinators of

all sorts. Pollination is essential to human life in so many ways. She then told me she firmly believes that someday all the world's food will come from high-rise hydroponic farms and that we'll probably just invent some kind of robotic pollination system, so we can surely survive without bugs of any sort.

I wanted to laugh out loud, but instead I mentioned what I like to call the poop factor. Who is going to get rid of all the waste in the world if there aren't any insects? Then I mentioned the food chain factor: insects are undeniably responsible for nearly all the food we eat, even the animals (are they to be grown in high-rise laboratories, too?). And then, of course, there's the whole air-we-breathe factor, which she clearly had not considered at all. My reply was something like, "If we don't have bugs, we don't have plants of any sort, and if we don't have plants, bye-bye oxygen. No oxygen, no humans." Don't get me wrong—I love a good debate. But there's no debate here. We need bugs.

But we've also got some problems with them that will probably never be sorted out. As you already know, fewer than 1 percent of insects are considered agricultural pests, but those that *are* present some big challenges. As we continue to turn to more ecologically friendly methods of pest control, the use of natural enemies to aid our efforts becomes more and more valuable. The science of biological control, or biocontrol, uses one living organism

Intentional beneficial insect releases are one element of biocontrol, the practice of using one living organism to help control the population of another.

to help control the population of another. After implementing the ideas presented in this book, you'll be practicing a few different biocontrol tactics in your own yard.

The first is conservation biological control. This refers to protecting and promoting the natural enemies already existing in your landscape by reducing or eliminating pesticides and by creating a more favorable habitat. Conservation biological control through habitat modification is essentially the act of building a landscape to enhance the numbers and actions of natural enemies. It is also possible to practice biocontrol through intentional insect releases (often referred to as augmentation), though unless you are releasing the insects into a contained environment, this type of biocontrol is only temporary. The intentional importation of natural enemies is a practice I'll discuss in a later chapter.

Another type of biological control, known as classic biocontrol, is not practiced by farmers or gardeners but rather by governmental agencies and universities. It refers to the intentional introduction of an insect predator or parasitoid to combat a particular pest. Classic biocontrol techniques are meant to be self-sustaining and permanent. (Remember what Joseph Patt told us about the parasitic wasp from Asia being considered for release in the United States to control the Asian citrus psyllid? That's an example of classic biocontrol.)

Though the term *biocontrol* might sound like something a terrorist is involved in, I can assure you that it is, in fact, a very useful (and definitely underappreciated) tool for gardeners and farmers. Since we already discussed the importance of doing away with pesticides, the remainder of this book focuses on how to enhance your landscape to the benefit of insect predators and parasitoids.

planning your border

The ability of a particular insectary planting to support beneficials is dependent on many factors, including its location, size, and design. Let's consider each of these in turn.

It is important to create a structurally diverse environment capable of supporting insects of all sorts—all while keeping your own sense of aesthetics in place.

Location

Begin the process of designing your own insectary border by carefully considering the placement of the planting. Border location is important because some natural enemies, like hoverflies, larger parasitic wasps, tachinid flies, and robber flies, are capable of traveling great distances, while others, including ladybugs, ground and rove beetles, smaller parasitic wasps, and the larvae of many predators, are more likely to have a far smaller home range. There are two ways you

Incorporating individual beneficial insect–friendly plants into an existing landscape is a good way to get started.

can approach the creation of your border.

The first is to *not* consider it a dedicated border per se but rather to incorporate as many of the plants profiled in the previous chapter into your existing landscape as possible. Scattering them about in hopes of increasing the structural and floral diversity of your existing landscape will likely lead to an increase in the numbers and diversity of beneficials you find on your property. To some extent, this is how I got started with my own insectary plantings. I already had a handful of perennial gardens, a vegetable garden, and lots of shrub beds and foundation plantings. Instead of adding plants that I thought were pretty, I began to incorporate

some of the species known to provide for beneficials (many of which also happen to be very pretty plants). The addition of any of these plants to any part of your landscape is a decent place to start.

The second way to approach the creation of your insectary border is to do what I eventually did: purposefully design and install a proper insectary border. The placement of such a garden is only slightly trickier than the willy-nilly approach of individual plant additions. Wind and sun exposure should be a consideration here, as many of the appropriate plants require at least six to eight hours of full sun per day (not to mention that most good bugs also do their best work in full sun),

Select the location of your insectary border carefully, as many of the most desirable plants prefer six to eight hours of full sun per day. A slightly sheltered site is ideal for smaller beneficials that have difficulty flying in windy conditions.

and many smaller species of beneficials have difficulty flying in windy conditions and thus prefer a somewhat sheltered site.

Another factor influencing the placement of your border is its proximity to other garden areas. For example, if you are looking to increase the predation and parasitism rates of the pests in your veggie garden, consider locating your border in close proximity to it. Molecular gut-content analysis found phacelia pollen in the digestive systems of hoverflies as far as 200 meters (656 feet) from the plants themselves. That's a substantial distance. But just because we know that some predators and parasitoids are capable of traveling sizable distances, why force them to? Why risk their not returning to the veggie garden for prey after they visit the nectar-rich insectary border?

The closer a dedicated insectary border is to the targeted pests, the better. That being said, close is relative. If your yard is a quarter-acre lot, anyplace is a good place to locate an insectary border in terms of its proximity to pests; but if you have a larger property, think a bit more carefully about its placement.

Size and style

The size of your insectary border matters, too, though not as much as you might think. Yes, the area should be proportionate to the remainder of your landscape (if only for the sake of good design), but there's really no need to overthink the garden's size in regard to its benefits to natural enemies. Covering just 1 percent of a given home landscape area with insectary plantings is a good initial target.

The targeted 1 percent can come in the form of a single insectary border positioned judiciously, or it can be the result of several smaller insectary beds dotted here and there, perhaps in relation to pest-prone areas. For a 1-acre lot, this translates to a single 20-by-20-foot (6-by-6-meter) border, or a similarly sized 400-square-foot (37-square-meter) area. For a quarter-acre lot, a single 10-by-10-foot (3-by-3-meter) border, or a similarly sized 200-square-foot (18.5-square-meter) area would suffice. While this may seem a rather large area to plant and maintain, don't forget that included in the desired 1 percent are also any areas that already contain insect-friendly plants. This means that if insectary plants are incorporated somehow into the rest of your landscape, the size of your dedicated insectary border can be reduced by an equal amount. Keep in mind, though, that there are no rules about all this—only

Covering just 1 percent of your property with insectary plantings is a good initial target. And because many insectary plants are very attractive, using them as part of a foundation planting adds color, texture, and complexity to what is often an uninteresting part of the landscape.

the suggested objective of doing whatever you can to increase the habitat available for natural enemies.

Depending on your garden style, an insectary border can be formally constructed, crisply edged, and precisely designed; or it can be a casual blend with no formal design, minimal maintenance, and riotous color. Fitting the overall design of an insectary border into the scope and attitude of your existing landscape style is a must. Otherwise, it will appear to be plunked there—an afterthought of sorts.

lessons for the home gardener from farmscaping

Based on an interview with Rex Dufour, entomologist and director of the Davis, California, branch office of the National Center for Appropriate Technology, which oversees the National Sustainable Agriculture Information Service

An insectary strip of buckwheat is planted in a field adjacent to an orchard.

FARMSCAPING, LIKE CREATING an insectary border but on a far larger scale, is "the thoughtful manipulation of a collection of plants intended to provide resources for predators, parasites, and other beneficials year-round," according to Rex Dufour. Meant to encourage biodiversity on a farm, farmscaping integrates insectary plantings, hedgerows, and cover crops into a whole-farm approach intended to support any and all natural enemies present. Insectary plantings, borders, or strips are incorporated side by side with market crops in order to naturally enhance predation and parasitism rates. Home gardeners can learn a thing or two from farmscaping strategies.

Dufour suggests that farmers begin the farmscaping process by thinking about which natural enemies they want to encourage based on which pests they are trying to control. Then they can design their insectary plantings to reflect those needs. For example, intercropping lettuce with insectary plants such as sweet alyssum is standard practice on organic lettuce farms in parts of California. Those plants are selected specifically to attract hoverflies, the larvae of which are predators of lettuce-sucking aphids. The result is fewer aphids. By the same token, home gardeners can think about the targeted pest, the desired natural enemies, and insectary plants that will attract those enemies.

Many different strategies, some more intensive than others, are employed in the practice of farmscaping. A simple plan might include strips of beneficial insect–supporting cover crops like alfalfa and buckwheat (both provide much-coveted extrafloral nectar supplies along with shelter) between crop rows. It might also include letting lettuce or mustard plants go to flower after the harvest, since these flowers are good pollen and nectar sources for the

Farmscaping plans can be as simple as incorporating strips of beneficial insect-supporting cover crops like alfalfa between crop rows.

it's safe to say the closer the insectary plants are to the crop they're intended to protect, the better. Covering 3 to 5 percent of a field area with scattered strips or blocks of insectary plantings provides enough general habitat for a broad range of natural enemies. The overwintering sites provided by these dedicated, scattered insectary plantings also ensure carryover of natural enemies from one year to the next. Dufour suggests that farmers turn little patches of otherwise unused land—areas around irrigation ditches, embankments, fence lines, and corners of fields—into islands of biodiversity by planting natural enemy friendly plants there. The home gardener can do the same, keeping in mind Dufour's caution that it's important to manage weeds in insectary plantings until the intended plants can take hold.

Farmscaping, like incorporating insectary plants in the home garden, also presents the opportunity for secondary crop production. Many of the flowering plants known to support beneficials also have other uses. Culinary herbs such as oregano, cilantro, anise, dill, and fennel can be planted for insectary habitat and also harvested for use or sale. Cut flowers are another possible secondary crop. Angelica, bishop's flower, yarrow, and others make bright, salable bouquets.

"You need to ensure that the plants selected for the insectary plantings don't serve as alternate hosts for other pest or disease organisms," warns Dufour. In California, pesty

next cycle of natural enemies. A slightly more complex plan might involve adding strips of an annual flowering insectary plant blend or perennial perimeter plantings around crop fields. The most complex farmscaping plans may involve introducing permanent windbreaks, ground covers, and hedgerows to both provide physical habitats for beneficials and increase the ecological diversity and architectural complexity of the farm. Plans for insectary plantings in a home garden can be similarly simple or complex, or anywhere in between.

The placement of any insectary plantings may depend on the targeted natural enemy, but

This farm in Oregon is using sunflowers and calendula to attract the true bug predators that prey on onion thrips.

insectary border, you are going to encourage more predators and parasitoids than pests.

Although it can be hard to quantify just exactly how natural enemies impact the numbers of any given pest, many studies show that biodiversity is greater on organic farms than on conventional ones and that that diversity provides a great system of checks and balances. Just as in a home garden, a diverse habitat is better equipped to handle any pest issues that come along.

Research at Virginia Tech supports the importance of insectary plantings by examining insect numbers in relation to farmscaping practices. Test plots were installed in 2004 and incorporated a combination of broccoli and squash plants with insectary species, including coriander, phacelia, yarrow, bishop's flower, chamomile, sweet alyssum, cosmos, and many others. Described as an "unqualified success," the farmscaping practices implemented resulted in reliable yields and increased numbers of many natural enemies.

The implementation of farmscaping practices requires both patience and adaptation—what works for one farmer may not work for another. Farmscaping will not eliminate pests from the farm, nor should it. When properly employed, however, it works to keep pest numbers at a tolerable level and prevent future outbreaks. The same can be said of the insectary border in the home landscape.

lygus bugs sometimes partake of the pollen and nectar offered by the coyote brush and native buckwheats planted in insectary plantings. But if you take care to choose the right plants for your

Design

Once you've decided on the site, size, and style of your border, begin making a few casual drawings of the anticipated bed in reference to the existing landscape and the structures already on your property. Keep things to scale if possible (large graph paper might help).

First draw the outline of the house, garage, shed, pool, and any other structures. You don't have to be a perfectionist by any means, but getting a rough idea of existing curves and angles is helpful. Then draw in any existing gardens, beds, and borders. Examine their edges and aim to create your new insectary border with a complementary framework. If your landscape has lots of soft curves, edge your insectary border with one too. If sharp, angular corners abound, then stick with them and build a more rectangular insectary border. Experiment on the paper with different bed shapes, sizes, and angles. Invest in a good eraser—you might need it.

After settling on the basic geometrical design of the border, turn to plant selection. Sort through the plant profiles in the previous chapter, making note of which are appropriate for your hardiness zone, which are must-haves, and which are I-think-nots. Once you've compiled a list of desired plants, categorize them based on bloom time. Without a doubt, the central and most critical focus of plant selection here is staggered bloom times.

From the moment many natural enemies emerge from their winter rest, they need to begin to feed. Without early nectar sources present, the insects commute to find suitable forage and might not return to your landscape (especially if it is a species capable of distance travel). Nectar, pollen, and prey need to be available throughout the entire season and right up to the point where overwintering insects enter diapause. In warmer climes, this means organizing the garden so that several different insectary plants are flowering year-round.

Both flower and plant structure are significant here as well. Vary the bed's architectural matrix by introducing plants of differing heights, girths, and frames. The diversity factor comes into play big time here. Don't settle

An insectary planting like this one is intentionally created to provide for the environmental and nutritional needs of a vast array of natural enemies.

A diversity of flower shapes and bloom times is critical for enhancing both the aesthetic appeal of the garden and its ability to support a broad range of natural enemies.

for only members of the same plant family with similar floral architecture. Incorporate a mixture of shallow, tubular flowers with daisy-like ray flowers and tiny, delicate umbels. Look to flower and foliage color, too, as the combinations should be suited to your taste, but the objective of diversity needs to take the lead.

Use your on-paper design to fiddle with different plant layout scenarios if you'd like, though this is not a step I usually do myself. Since I have trouble envisioning a three-dimensional garden via a two-dimensional plan, I like to work within the bed itself. However, I do use the written plan to determine the approximate number of plants I'll need to adequately fill the space (this is where the mature plant size measurements I provide in the plant profiles come in handy). Suitable plant spacing is necessary not only for the health of the plants but also to facilitate insect movement. Place the plants too close and they outcompete each other; place them too far apart and smaller natural enemies may have a hard time scooting from plant to plant to find suitable food and prey.

Once I determine the number and types of plants I want to include, I buy them and then head to the garden to determine their placement. I place the plants, pot and all, and then move them around as I see fit. In my mind, I visualize their mature size, flower structure, and color at maturity, and work to pair them with neighboring plants in a way that appeals to both my own sense of aesthetics and the needs of all my beneficial bugs. The good news is that if I don't like something down the line, it's easy enough to change simply by shuffling things around.

Look to include appealing color combinations in your border but also keep varied floral structures in mind. This combination of oregano, asters, and laceflower partners small, tubular flowers with daisylike flowers and tiny, shallow umbels.

insectary garden plans

Planning your border may be easier for you if you have some models to follow, so I provide four different insectary garden designs here. Within each design are all the desired elements—staggered bloom times, diverse floral and plant architecture, and visual appeal. All the plans are also easily size-adaptable—you'll note that they lack dimensions. That's so that you can shrink or expand the bed according to the amount of space you have available simply by adjusting the number of plants to locate in each position. Bigger areas will allow for three or four of some of the plants noted on the plan, while smaller spaces may have room for only one specimen. There is also quite a bit of wiggle room regarding flower color and cultivar selections. I purposely left out cultivar names so that you can choose them based on what is most attractive to you in regard to color combinations and growth habits.

A Simple Annual Insectary Bed

Having only a weekend's worth of spare time shouldn't stop you from creating beneficial insect–friendly habitat around your home. This simple plan is designed to fit into the confines of a single raised bed, built either from a purchased kit or from scratch using lumber, rocks, or bricks to create the frame. Heck, you can even create this plan without the raised bed. Just plant it straight into the ground—it's that simple. Each of the ten plants included in this plan is an annual, which means they'll grow quickly and be inexpensive to install (all can be started from seed sown directly into the garden or from transplants).

I selected these plants to provide for a miscellany of natural enemies. The range of floral structures is designed to support them all—from the tiniest parasitic wasp and minute pirate bug to the thumbnail-size syrphid fly, and everything in between. Because it consists exclusively of annuals, this simple design is suited to a huge range of gardening climates and is easily modified from year to year if necessary. That being said, all of the annuals in this plan readily self-sow. Allowing them to drop some seed each year means a perpetually self-planting garden that comes back every spring all on its own. You'll only need to thin the resulting seedlings (if they come up too thickly) and weed, mulch, and water it from time to time. This plan is as easy as it gets.

Plant list
1. sunflowers (*Helianthus annuus*)
2. sweet alyssum (*Lobularia maritima*)
3. dill (*Anethum graveolens*)
4. cosmos (*Cosmos bipinnatus*)
5. cilantro/coriander (*Coriandrum sativum*)
6. annual black-eyed Susan (*Rudbeckia hirta*)
7. annual tickseed (*Coreopsis tinctora*)
8. toothpickweed (*Ammi visnaga*)
9. sweet alyssum (*Lobularia maritima*)
10. Roman chamomile (*Anthemis nobilis*)

Plant list
1. tomatoes
2. zucchini
3. mustard greens
4. sweet alyssum (*Lobularia maritima*)
5. chervil (*Anthriscus cerefolium*)
6. lettuce
7. carrots
8. Roman chamomile (*Anthemis nobilis*)
9. onions
10. zinnias
11. eggplant
12. broccoli
13. cosmos (*Cosmos bipinnatus*)
14. cabbage
15. parsley (*Petroselinum crispum*)
16. basil
17. beets
18. bush beans
19. eggplant
20. sunflowers (*Helianthus annuus*)
21. horsemint (*Monarda punctata*)
22. thyme
23. sage
24. fennel
25. oregano (*Origanum vulgare*)
26. dill (*Anethum graveolens*)

A Vegetable Insectary Garden

Without insect-friendly flowering plants, beneficial insects may be less likely to call your veggie patch home—and that, of course, means they'll be less likely to help control all the pests living there. A good vegetable garden design, like this one, incorporates the crops you want to grow as well as a diversity of flowers capable of satisfying the nutritional needs of a broad range of natural enemies. These annual and perennial flowering plants not only provide nectar for natural enemies but also represent a great food source for pollinators, luring more of them to the garden where they'll also do a fine job of boosting the yields of your zucchini, beans, and other crops.

Because most gardeners turn over the soil in their vegetable garden each year, this plan incorporates mostly flowering annuals so that at season's end you can toss them into the compost pile with your tomato vines and bolted lettuce. However, there should also be a more permanent place for some of the natural enemies to take shelter during times when the rest of the garden is fallow. This is where the central bed comes in. Here you'll notice a number of perennial herbs that should be left to stand through the winter months. This area is not to be tilled or otherwise disturbed, and while these herbs can certainly be harvested in the spring for kitchen use, they should then be allowed to come into flower for the benefit of nectar- and pollen-eating parasitoids, predators, and pollinators.

When tailoring this plan to your own site, keep in mind that there is great flexibility regarding the vegetables you can grow in each specific area. Substitutions are expected. However, no matter which vegetables you choose to plant, sticking with a collection of flowering plants similar to the one highlighted in this plan is a good idea. This group of insectary plants represents a broad range of floral structures, plant heights, and growth habits, and about as much bloom-time diversity as you can get among an assemblage of flowering annuals. Most are easily started from seed, making a plan like this both easy on the gardening budget and tough on pests.

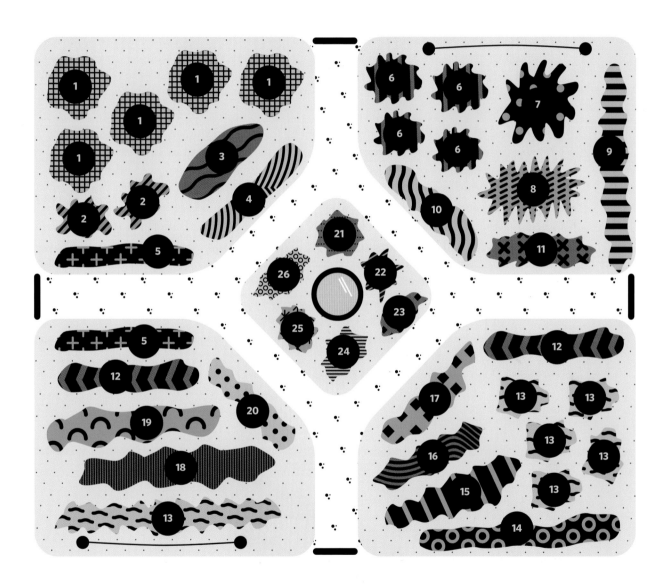

• •

A Woody Ornamental Insectary Bed

In my mind, the ubiquitous shrub island holds the greatest untapped potential for beneficial insect habitat. As you'll recall, the tree canopy and ground cover layers seem to be the most valuable landscape strata for supporting insects of all sorts. Right now, a drive down a typical suburban street reveals that most shrub islands are rather desolate places, carved out of the lawn and containing a single tree, perhaps with one or two neighboring shrubs. A handful of impatiens or begonias might find a home there in the summertime. The whole thing is then smothered in mulch and surrounded by a sea of lawn.

But what if we combined these existing tree and shrub layers with levels of herbaceous flowering plants and ground covers? For when the tree canopy is partnered with as many other vegetation layers as possible,

that is when we see the greatest numbers of natural enemies. Changing our desolate shrub islands to islands of biodiversity is putting the proverbial icing on the cake. It is making the most of an already existing space, easily turning it into a place where beneficial insects can take shelter, find food, and lay eggs—in short, where they can make themselves at home.

This garden plan is aimed at creating precisely such a home. It incorporates a multitude of vegetative layers, floral structures, bloom times, and growth habits. Pairing a small specimen tree with flowering shrubs and several herbaceous ornamentals fulfills both the nutritional and the environmental needs of any resident beneficial insects. The noted flexibility on the shrub choices makes the plan suitable to a broad range of gardening climates.

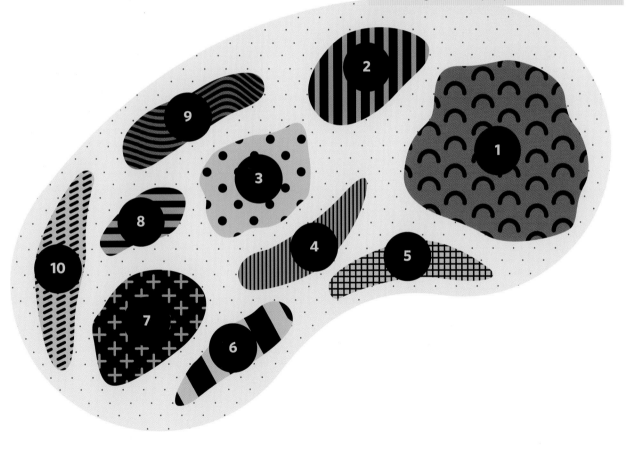

Plant list

1. small tree of your choice
2. green-headed coneflower (*Rudbeckia laciniata*)
3. shrubby cinquefoil (*Dasiphora fruticosa* subsp. *floribunda*) or coyote brush (*Baccharis pilularis*)
4. Shasta daisy (*Leucanthemum ×superbum*)
5. lacy phacelia (*Phacelia tanacetifolia*)
6. golden alexanders (*Zizia aurea*)
7. steeplebush (*Spiraea tomentosa*) or hardhack steeple bush (*Spiraea douglasii*)
8. yarrow (*Achillea millefolium*)
9. boneset (*Eupatorium perfoliatum*)
10. New England aster (*Symphyotrichum novae-angliae*)

A Modular Insectary Plan

Many other areas of a home landscape have the potential to become suitable locations for insectary plantings. From front walkways and mailbox gardens, to foundation plantings and perennial borders, as long as a particular site receives six to eight hours of full sun per day, it is a possible candidate. And if it is sheltered from high winds, all the better.

In hopes of making it easy for you to convert any new or existing garden space into an insectary border, I offer you a modular plan—one that can be tailored to fit into nearly any garden area by repeating its pattern of plant combinations any number of times as necessary. It comprises a group of plants that in partnership with each other provide all the necessary qualities of an effective insectary border.

Use it to renovate or adapt an existing bed into an insectary border. Repeat its pattern along road frontage or down a fence line. Border your yard to create a shared habitat between yourself and a neighbor (or to separate your yard from your neighbor's). Replicate the plan over and over until you have concealed an aboveground pool or a dog run. Line both sides of your driveway, get rid of your lawn, cover the entire yard. Use it however you see fit. That's what it was designed for.

Plant list
1. Culver's root (*Veronicastrum virginicum*)
2. sunflower (*Helianthus annuus*)
3. boltonia (*Boltonia asteroides* var. *latisquama*)
4. blue vervain (*Verbena hastata*)
5. lovage (*Levisticum officinale*)
6. purplestem angelica (*Angelica atropurpurea*)
7. Canada goldenrod (*Solidago canadensis*)
8. meadowsweet (*Spiraea alba*) or hardhack steeplebush (*Spiraea douglasii*)
9. lanceleaf coreopsis (*Coreopsis lanceolata*)
10. smooth oxeye (*Heliopsis helianthoides*)
11. Shasta daisy (*Leucanthemum ×superbum*)
12. yellow coneflower (*Ratibida pinnata*)
13. brown-eyed Susan (*Rudbeckia triloba*)
14. shrubby cinquefoil (*Dasiphora fruticosa* subsp. *floribunda*)
15. short-toothed mountain mint (*Pycnanthemum muticum*)
16. heartleaf golden alexanders (*Zizia aptera*)
17. yarrow (*Achillea millefolium*)
18. anise (*Pimpinella anisum*)
19. aster (*Symphyotrichum* species)
20. calamint (*Calamintha* species)
21. wallflower (*Erysimum* species)
22. basket of gold (*Aurinia saxatilis*)
23. oregano (*Origanum vulgare*)

installing and maintaining the insectary border

Before planting your border, take the time to create good growing conditions. As many of the plants you'll be growing there do indeed require half-decent soil, spend some time considering the conditions of your site. The large majority of insectary plants featured throughout this book do best in average garden soil. No matter your soil type, additions of compost or well-aged animal manure improve soil structure, amend drainage issues, and serve to add various nutrients. As many of the best plants for beneficials actually prefer leaner soils, there is generally no need to add supplemental granular fertilizers. A few inches of compost each year is adequate.

Beginning your insectary border from scratch can be quite a challenge. If you have any reservations about your physical ability to create a new planting bed, you may want to consider hiring someone to do this part for you (and that is precisely what my husband and I have done ever since using a torturous sod-cutter to create a new planting bed at our farm). If you do decide to prepare the planting bed yourself, be aware that after any sod is stripped, the site should be tilled and a few inches of organic matter should be added before planting. There is also the "pile-it-on-and-wait" method, which involves placing 1 to 2 feet of well-aged animal manure, shredded leaves, grass clippings, compost, or even newspaper and unwaxed corrugated cardboard in layers over the bed to essentially smother the turf and, over time (you may have to wait six months to a year), amend the soil.

Or build a raised bed—one method capable of generating your new insectary border with a single weekend's effort. Plenty of do-it-yourself frame kits are available these days that snap together and don't even require tools. Or if you are handy, you can build your own frame with rot-resistant locust, cedar, or redwood planks. Stacked rocks, blocks, and bricks are good options, too. Once the frame is built, fill the bed with a mixture of three-quarters garden soil (or carefully sourced topsoil if you don't have any extra soil from your own property) and one-quarter screened compost. It's ready to plant in just a few hours.

After your border has been installed, it needs to be maintained. Don't be fooled into thinking an insectary border is no-maintenance. It certainly can be (that is, if you are OK with weeds and don't mind things running amok), but in most cases the insectary border is maintained much like any other garden area. How well it is maintained, of course, depends as much on the gardener's control issues as it does on the plants selected to grow there. Watering is necessary, at least until the garden is well established; and once or twice a year, things need to be cut back. But that's the bare minimum.

Beyond that, you decide whether to religiously deadhead any spent flowers, weed to your heart's content, mulch annually, and canoodle around in there as much as you see fit. Or you can choose to do nothing. My own maintenance requirements fall somewhere in between. I deadhead my insectary border once in mid to late summer (in hopes of encouraging further blooms), mulch it with a few inches of leaf compost in spring (in hopes of discouraging weeds), weed it a few times a year (because the mulching never works as well as I want it to), and cut it down and clean it up each spring. Otherwise I let it be. Disturbing the natural enemies there is not something I desire; I think they do their best work when they are left alone.

You may have noticed that I mentioned cutting down and cleaning up the border each *spring*. This is something most folks tend to do in the fall, but it's far better for your bugs to hold off on this duty until late the following spring. Remember, an insectary border doesn't serve just as a nutritional source for beneficials; it also provides greatly needed overwintering habitat. When we cover our yards with a monoculture of grass and just a smattering of evergreens and flowering shrubs, and collect every fallen leaf and twig, we essentially eliminate the sheltered sites that insects of all

Maintaining your insectary garden requires as much, or as little, work as you desire. Just don't cut down your insectary plantings in the fall, as they provide much-needed overwintering habitat to many beneficials.

sorts rely on to see themselves safely through the winter months.

Though I probably can't convince you to return your yard to its prehuman native state (nor do I think it's even feasible), I do encourage you to allow your insectary border to stand as is through the winter. The leaves and dead stems collected there serve as critical good bug habitat. In my opinion, they also add texture and interest to what may otherwise be a very bland winter landscape.

companion planting

battling pests with plant partnerships

One field of study garnering a lot of attention from entomologists these days is the idea of companion planting for pest control. With scores of studies already conducted and many more under way, this research stands to provide enormous benefits to growers of all sizes in respect to managing pest insects without the excessive use of pesticides. Our knowledge of these techniques is constantly evolving as new studies emerge, but the general concepts of companion planting already play an important role in the management of agricultural pests and will no doubt continue to do so in the future.

As a gardener, you are probably already familiar with the core concept of companion planting. In essence, it is the partnering of two or more plant species in order to provide

Pairing beneficial insect-attracting flowers with vegetables is just one way companion planting can promote a balanced landscape. The pests provide the protein, and the flowering herbs and other plants incorporated via companion planting provide the necessary carbohydrates.

Companion planting can be used to maximize available space. Growing pole beans up corn plants is one way to take advantage of different architectural layers as well as to utilize the nitrogen-fixing capabilities of the bean plants to help enrich the soil.

as a diversionary tactic as well; perhaps one of the plants has a strong odor that works to mask the desirable plant from pests or to otherwise conceal it. And companion planting is used to lure pests away from intended crops in a practice known as trap cropping. Once the targeted pests are gathered on their preferred plant, the trap crop, they are destroyed.

From saving space and fixing nitrogen to repelling pests from plants and luring them to trap crops, companion planting techniques are no doubt useful to the farmers and gardeners who employ them. The rest of this chapter is dedicated to a different facet of companion planting—creating plant partnerships that serve to recruit, protect, and provide for natural enemies of all sorts. The insectary borders soon to be incorporated into your landscape are, in fact, a form of companion planting, but other companion planting techniques exist that can benefit natural enemies and perhaps prove a valuable tool for increasing their numbers. My goal here is to shed some light on companion planting as it relates to beneficials, as well as to outline a few other opportunities gardeners and farmers have to provide for the needs of all their predators and parasitoids.

how companion planting works to deter pests

One of the most interesting studies I have read was from a pair of researchers in the United

some benefit to the plants themselves and, as a result, to the grower. The plant species involved are typically grown in close physical proximity to each other or as succession crops.

Gardeners and farmers use companion planting techniques for several different reasons. First, these techniques maximize available space by taking advantage of different growing layers—for example, growing vine crops up a fence and planting low-growing herbs around their feet to save space. Companion planting is also sometimes aimed at providing for a particular nutritional need, as is the case when planting nitrogen-fixing legumes or leguminous cover crops alongside, or prior to planting, nitrogen-hungry crops. Companion planting is frequently employed

Interplanting a vegetable garden with a diversity of species and numerous flowering plants may serve not only to attract natural enemies but also to make it more difficult for pest insects to find their desired host plant.

host plant (cabbage) before settling down to lay eggs.

The researchers noted that the pest insects in their study needed to make a specific number of appropriate landings on the desired plant's foliage before receiving enough stimuli to start laying eggs. When the cabbage plants were undersown with a companion planting of clover, the pests inevitably ended up occasionally landing on the clover, messing up the number of appropriate landings on the cabbage and making it less likely that they would settle down to lay eggs on or near the intended host plants. The mere presence of the clover was enough to disrupt their egg-laying behaviors. It was noted that 36 percent of the observed cabbage root flies laid eggs near cabbages grown in bare soil while only 7 percent laid eggs on those plants surrounded by clover.

Though this theory of appropriate/inappropriate landings needs further study, it is a concept that could have a significant impact on the way we grow edible plants. On a typical farm, where crops are grown in large monocultures, the chances of a pest insect making the required number of appropriate landings is huge; nothing else is growing there for them to land on, after all. But on farms and in home gardens that work to integrate biodiversity-enhancing techniques, pest insects may, in fact, have a harder time finding host plants. It also explains in part why certain herbivorous

Kingdom who proposed that plant-munching pests find host plants not only through visual cues and volatile chemical signals (or odors) produced by the host plants themselves, but also by making a series of landings on the plant's foliage and tasting it with receptors on their feet. This hypothesis is based on observations of herbivorous insects (cabbage root flies) making a series of landings on the

Interspersing preferred host plants with other plants may serve to divert pests. On a farm, this might mean alternating crop rows, while in a home vegetable garden, simply pumping up the species diversity serves a similar purpose.

insects are pests in an agricultural setting but not in the diverse settings of a natural habitat.

To increase your chances of integrating successful insectary companion plantings into your landscape, it's important to look for profitable partnerships between plants and the beneficial insects they support. Many examples exist of this type of companion planting. A few that I think are well suited to gardeners for their ease of application, effectiveness, and attractiveness are interplanting, cover cropping, planting sunflowers, incorporating herbs in the vegetable garden, and creating hedgerows and beetle bumps. Let's look at each of these concepts in turn.

interplanting

It stands to reason that it is far easier for an herbivore to become abundant when the resources it needs to survive are concentrated in one particular area. But when the preferred host plants are interspersed with other plants,

Combining pepper plants with dill provided my neighbor the benefits of both the natural enemies the dill attracted to the garden and two harvestable crops to sell at market.

Interplanting is done in several ways. On a large scale, it entails various farmscaping techniques, including planting different crops in alternating rows, but in the smaller scale of a home garden, it could involve something as simple as underplanting your tomatoes with a mixture of lettuce and sweet alyssum. The tomatoes shade the lettuce from the summer sun, while the alyssum lures in the parasitic wasps that control the aphids on the lettuce. In my own garden, I get higher yields because I am making good use of all the space in my garden, and I have fewer weeds because the alyssum and lettuce form a living mulch beneath the tomatoes. An old neighbor used to interplant his rows of peppers and eggplants with rows of dill and coriander. He sold the herbs at market but also enjoyed the benefits of the natural enemies these plants brought to his garden when they came into flower.

pest densities are reduced. The technique known as interplanting, or intercropping, serves to break up resource concentrations and divert pests. It involves growing several different crops together to increase structural diversity, create a more favorable habitat for beneficials, and build corridors for insect migration to and from crops. Interplanting is known to increase the number of predators and parasitoids not only by introducing diversity but also by adding potential nectar and pollen sources and alternate prey for these insects.

cover cropping

If you are a vegetable gardener or farmer, cover cropping stands to play a huge role in increasing the diversity of the beneficial insects found on your property. Depending on the plant species, cover crops can provide much coveted extrafloral nectar. Flowering cover crops like legumes, alfalfa, clovers, and buckwheat serve as a nectar source for beneficials, and cover crops of mixed species extend the flowering season through their bloom

Cover crops like crimson clover add organic matter to the soil as well as supporting many species of natural enemies, particularly during the winter months.

Sunflowers begin to increase the populations of certain beneficials when they are a mere 6 inches high. The production of both floral and extrafloral nectar makes them very valuable to nectar-seeking predators and parasitoids like these soldier beetles.

succession and provide nectar for beneficials when prey are scarce. Cover crops help see many beneficials through the winter months by providing undisturbed shelter, and their mere presence leads to increased populations of natural enemies in early spring.

Cases in point: a two-year study in Georgia found that the population of big-eyed bugs was significantly higher in cotton fields previously planted in crimson clover as opposed to those fields allowed to lie fallow before the cotton was planted. The same study found that ladybugs commuted from cover crops into crop fields. In Hawaii, a cover crop of buckwheat interplanted with zucchini reduced whiteflies and aphids, and broccoli interplanted with a cover crop of yellow sweet clover showed reduced populations of imported cabbage worms and cabbage loopers.

The benefits of cover crops extend well beyond their ability to support natural enemies, of course. They reduce soil erosion, add organic matter to the soil, increase fertility, filter pollution, and suppress weeds. You should be aware, however, that some cover crops actually attract specific pests. For example, crimson clover may draw tarnished plant bugs, and a combination of clover and mixed legumes has been shown to attract several species of pest stink bugs (which can be a good thing if your aim is to also use the cover crop as a trap crop intended to keep the stink bugs away from desired plantings). Though cover crops do far more good than harm in terms of luring insects to the landscape, this is certainly something you want to avoid. Before deciding which cover crops to plant at your house, contact the experts at your local agricultural extension for their advice.

Sunflowers planted in orchards attract many of the beneficial insects that prey upon common orchard pests. They are also being investigated as a trap crop for brown marmorated stink bugs in orchards.

planting sunflowers

Sunflowers are desirable insectary plants, and including them in your insectary border is a great idea. But you can also use them as companion plants to really lure in the beneficials. As they produce extrafloral nectar in addition to floral nectar, they are known to attract beneficials when the plants are still very small. Researchers have noted an increase in the population levels of various predaceous natural enemies when the plants reach a mere 6 inches high. Though the population density of these beneficials is highest on the sunflower plants themselves, the insects do indeed travel several yards away from the plants to seek prey and hosts for their young. Planting sunflowers within rows of vegetables is an effective way to attract more beneficials, though care must be taken to select a location where the sunflowers won't shade sun-loving crops.

Research is being conducted regarding using sunflowers as a trap crop for the recently introduced brown marmorated stink bug in orchards. Regardless of the outcome of that research, sunflowers are an excellent companion plant to orchard trees. They attract many of the insects that prey upon common orchard pests. Plant rows of sunflowers between orchard rows or, in the home garden, plant groupings of sunflowers around individual trees or around the perimeter of home orchards. Do keep in mind, though, that

Incorporating both annual and perennial flowering herbs into the vegetable garden means better support for your resident natural enemies.

This hedgerow of hardhack (*Spiraea douglasii*) in Washington state serves to provide beneficials with a nectar source, alternative insect prey or hosts, and permanent, year-round habitat.

the height of larger sunflower varieties may surpass that of many dwarf trees so that the sunflowers compete with the trees for water, nutrients, and light. Be sure to choose appropriate varieties to avoid this situation.

incorporating herbs in the vegetable garden

An integrated vegetable garden—one that incorporates an array of flowering plants with the vegetables themselves—is another excellent way to diversify the garden and provide for a wide range of predators and parasitoids. It also makes for a beautiful garden. Several of the best nectar sources for smaller species of beneficials are plants commonly grown as culinary herbs. A very useful companion planting technique is to incorporate these herbs right into the vegetable garden. They can readily be harvested for kitchen use, and later in the season, when they are left to flower, they provide beneficials with nectar and pollen.

My own garden is designed with a large oval-shaped bed at its center. The bed is permanent and filled with a variety of both perennial and annual herbs. I harvest and dry my perennial herbs, including chives, oregano, sage, thyme, and fennel, several times throughout the spring and then allow them to flower when summer arrives. I also plant several annual and biennial herbs in this bed, as well as in various places throughout the garden, again with the goal of eventually letting them come into flower. Included in this list are cilantro, chervil, basil, dill, and parsley.

creating hedgerows

Many species of beneficials are known to prefer the type of habitat provided by woody plants over that provided by annual and herbaceous plants. Some studies have shown that the diversity of parasitoids is highest on trees and shrubs. This is not only because these plants support many other insects that can be

beetle banks
(and bumps!)

Based on an interview with Gwendolyn Ellen, program manager of the Farmscaping for Beneficials Project, Oregon State University, Corvallis, Oregon

ORGANIC FARMERS ARE mandated by the rules of the USDA's National Organic Program to work to conserve biodiversity on their farms. Gwendolyn Ellen's job is to work with both organic and conventional farmers and with researchers to find ways to make this happen. In the early 2000s, Ellen and other scientists at Oregon State University began to develop a program to establish and study beetle banks. A regular practice of farmers in Great Britain and Australia, beetle banking involves creating elongated, semi-permanent raised berms throughout crop fields and planting them with grasses. Beetle banks are a great example of how habitat creation and companion planting can encourage populations of a very important predator.

Ellen explains that the predaceous ground beetles these banks are meant to encourage instinctively climb upward to stay high and dry, away from moisture. To encourage this natural behavior, beetle banks are raised a foot higher than ground level. The native bunch grasses planted on the banks provide a drier, warmer habitat for these insects during the winter.

The beetles especially like the organic matter that naturally accumulates around the base of these grasses. In the spring and summer, the beetles move out into the fields to forage for prey.

"You have to think like an insect," Ellen says. "Create a refuge from soil and pesticide disturbance. Our research shows that providing an undisturbed area, no matter what the size, increases the diversity of predaceous ground beetles on farms." Ellen's team encourages farmers to put in banks sized to fit with their farm's production practices and suggests incorporating a minimum of three different species of native bunch grasses (grass species that grow into a clump or tuft rather than spreading horizontally to form a sodlike mat) into a given beetle bank.

Why encourage ground beetles? Ellen calls them "a very important insect to have on a farm or garden" because they can hit pest insects as soil-dwelling pupae or larvae—a vulnerable stage. She explains that some species of ground beetles are specialized to reach up into snail shells to get out the goods or find and follow slug trails. Crawling around on the ground, they also eat slug and snail eggs.

Ellen and her team have worked with numerous farmers in Oregon to develop beetle banks in their orchards and vegetable fields. "Often farmers want to know how many beetles they can expect to colonize their banks and how many crop pests they are working to control. But we can't tell them these things because, with

A newly installed beetle bank has been planted with several species of native bunch grasses and mulched with straw.

This mature beetle bank on a farm in Oregon serves to support not only predaceous ground beetles but also many other beneficials.

insects, nothing is linear. Many of these beetles are opportunistic feeders and there are lots of factors affecting them, from the pesticides and fertilizers the farmer uses to the particular crops they're growing and even the weather." Still, Ellen's research has shown that when the banks are in place, a greater diversity of ground beetle species hang around. And they've found that these beetles aren't the only beneficials that use the banks. They are also finding rove beetles, ladybeetles, spiders, and lots of native bees.

For farmers, a good rule of thumb is to place one of these banks every 10 to 20 acres. Ellen suggests running the bank down the middle of a field because farms may already have undisturbed forested margins or grassy field edges. For home gardeners, she suggests creating what she calls beetle bumps—raised, circular areas in the lawn planted with multiple species of native bunch grasses. They don't have to be any particular shape or size; they just need to fit with your landscape.

Banks and bumps can be a year-round resource for beetles, and they can be aesthetically appealing as well, "like a little prairie in the middle of your farm or yard." Banks and bumps require very little maintenance. The areas need to be weeded until the grasses have established, and once a year they should be mowed or trimmed to a height of 6 to 8 inches. Mowing in the fall after the grasses have gone to seed will ensure a natural succession of new plants. Ellen recommends removing the grass straw from the banks or bumps after mowing to increase sunlight exposure and allow the area to dry out.

Plant your beetle bank or bump with regionally native grasses or cultivars of those species. Start the seeds indoors and then transplant the plants outside, or plant the grasses by heavy direct seeding in the fall.

used as hosts but also because they provide permanent, year-round habitat and possibly pollen and nectar. One way to increase the number of woody plants on your property is to install a hedgerow.

Hedgerows are linear, permanent plantings of a variety of trees, shrubs, and grasses. The plants are often closely spaced and selected to provide a succession of bloom throughout the season. Ideally, regionally native trees and shrubs with known appeal to beneficials anchor the hedgerow, while assorted native grasses and flowering perennials are added for diversity enhancement and curb appeal. Hedgerows can be planted on field edges, in orchards and vineyards, or simply along a property border. They are becoming increasingly popular for their ability to create protected, beneficial insect–friendly microclimates by reducing wind speed. But they can also help protect against erosion, filter airborne dust, shelter crops from winds and blowing snow, provide wildlife habitat, and increase pollinator diversity.

Evidence of hedgerows' ability to increase beneficial insect abundance and activity is building, though studies pinning down the exact extent of their capacity to do so are still in the works. A two-year study of several mature California hedgerows noted that 78 percent of the insects found living within them were beneficial, leading the researchers to conclude that these hedgerow plantings did enhance beneficial insect abundance and that such plantings may indeed help enhance biological pest control. In 2009 the USDA's Natural Resources Conservation Service (NRCS) helped California farmers install fifty-seven miles of hedgerows, and the practice is growing nationwide. The NRCS provides farmers with area-specific plant lists for building hedgerows as well as advice on establishing and maintaining them.

This Oregon hedgerow mixes ninebark (*Physocarpus* species) and mixed flowering plants.

putting it all together:
who the beneficials eat and what to plant

Many scientific studies have looked at various plants and what pests they deter based on the predators they are able to support, and you've already been introduced to some of the results in the plant profiles earlier in the book. Taking a little time to match up the targeted pest with a successful predator or parasitoid, and then with a plant or group of plants that can support that predator or parasitoid, can pay off in spades. This chart is intended to help you do just that.

beneficial insects	**assassin bugs**	**big-eyed bugs**
some of the pests they consume	Nearly any insect, including hornworms, Mexican bean beetles, Colorado potato beetles, leafhoppers, cucumber beetles, aphids, and caterpillars	Aphids, cabbage loopers, cabbage worms, caterpillars, cinch bugs, flea beetles, leafhoppers, lygus bug nymphs, corn earworms, beetles, spider mites, thrips, whiteflies, and the eggs of many pests
plants that support them	Both adults and nymphs are predaceous, so no particular flowers are preferred. A highly diverse habitat is best.	Big-eyed bugs will eat nectar and sap when prey are scarce. Cover crops like alfalfa and clover are good bets. Others include angelica, boltonia, buckwheat, caraway, cosmos, eriogonum, laceflower, sunflowers, and sweet alyssum.

damsel bugs

dragonflies and damselflies

Aphids, asparagus beetles, small caterpillars (including cabbage worms, tobacco budworms, and cutworms), Colorado potato beetle eggs and larvae, four-lined plant bugs, sawfly larvae, spider mites, whiteflies, and many other insects and eggs

Many insects, including mosquitoes, beetles, bees, ants, moths, and wasps

Both adults and nymphs are predaceous, so no particular flowers are preferred. A highly diverse habitat is best.

These insects do not rely on plants for nectar but do rely on them for habitat and as a source of prey. Increase plant diversity around ponds and streams by installing a buffer zone of plants.

beneficial insects	fireflies	ground beetles
some of the pests they consume	Snails, slugs, insect eggs, earthworms, and insect larvae	Asparagus beetles, caterpillars, Colorado potato beetles, corn earworms, cutworms, slugs, gypsy moth larvae, snails, squash vine borers, tobacco budworms, mites, aphids, snails, and caterpillars
plants that support them	Only larvae are predacious, so no particular flowers are preferred. Females prefer wet soil for egg laying. Do not fill in wetlands or low-lying areas. Provide plant diversity for best habitat.	Native bunch grasses provide the perfect habitat for these nocturnal beetles.

ladybugs

Aphids, asparagus beetle larvae, Colorado potato beetle larvae, lace bugs, mealybugs, bean beetle larvae, scale, spider mites, psyllids, adelgids, caterpillars, whiteflies and eggs, larvae and adults of several other pests

Both adult and larval ladybugs consume pests, but adults also need nectar and pollen. Plant anise, baccharis, boltonia, boneset, chamomile, cinquefoil, coriander, cosmos, cup plant, daisies, dill, eriogonum, feverfew, goldenrod, heliopsis, laceflower, lovage, meadowsweet, wallflower, and yellow coneflower.

lacewings

Aphids, asparagus beetle larvae, caterpillar eggs and young caterpillars, Colorado potato beetle larvae, corn earworms, lace bugs, some scales, whiteflies, spider mites, mealybugs, and various insect eggs

Plant angelica, anise, baccharis, calamint, caraway, coreopsis, coriander, cosmos, cup plant, daisies, eriogonum, feverfew, goldenrod, heliopsis, laceflower, lovage, mountain mint, oregano, sunflowers, sweet alyssum, verbena, wallflower, yarrow, and yellow coneflower

minute pirate bugs

Aphids, small caterpillars, lace bugs, Mexican bean beetle larvae, scales, spider mites, thrips, corn earworms, leafhoppers, psyllids, whiteflies, and various insect eggs

Early blooming plants are essential. Try alfalfa, asters, baccharis, basket of gold, boltonia, boneset, buckwheat, caraway, cinquefoil, coreopsis, coriander, crimson clover, Culver's root, cup plant, daisies, eriogonum, feverfew, goldenrod, laceflower, meadowsweet, oregano, verbena, wallflower, yarrow, and yellow coneflower.

beneficial insects	parasitic wasps	predatory mites
some of the pests they consume	Aphids, beetle larvae, bagworms, cabbage worms, Colorado potato beetles, corn earworms, cucumber beetles, cutworms, gypsy moth caterpillars, Japanese beetles, leafminers, mealybugs, bean beetles, sawfly larvae, squash vine borers, tent caterpillars, tobacco budworms, tomato hornworms, flies, scales, true bugs, and whiteflies	Pest mites, thrips, whiteflies, scale crawlers, leafhoppers, fungus gnats, and psyllids
plants that support them	Adult wasps need nectar and pollen. Plant angelica, anise, asters, baccharis, black-eyed Susan, boneset, buckwheat, caraway, chamomile, cilantro, cinquefoil, coreopsis, cosmos, Culver's root, daisies, eriogonum, golden alexanders, goldenrod, heliopsis, laceflower, lovage, meadowsweet, mountain mint, oregano, phacelia, sweet alyssum, verbena, yarrow, and yellow coneflower.	Predatory mites feed exclusively on other insects, so no particular plants will draw them in. Diverse habitat is best.

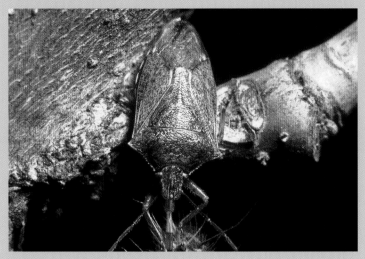

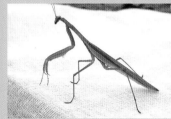

predatory stink bugs

praying mantids

Caterpillars, Japanese beetles, Mexican bean beetles, Colorado potato beetles, lygus bugs, beetle larvae, bollworms, and herbivorous stink bugs

Whatever they can catch, including moths, crickets, grasshoppers, flies, beetles, and caterpillars

Predatory stink bugs are most attracted to a landscape with plenty of cover and prey diversity.

Structural diversity is key, as is allowing plants to stand through the winter to shelter egg cases.

beneficial insects	 robber flies	 rove beetles	 syrphid flies
some of the pests they consume	Colorado potato beetles, four-lined plant bugs, grasshoppers, aphids, leafhoppers, Japanese beetles, Mexican bean beetles, and many others	Bark beetles, slugs, snails, ants, termites, root maggots, and other ground-dwelling pests	Aphids, young cabbage worms, thrips, leafhoppers, scales, mealybugs, and many small caterpillars.
plants that support them	Both robber fly adults and larvae are great predators. They are carnivorous and do not rely on plants for nourishment, so providing habitat is key. They prefer a diverse landscape filled with many different types of plants.	A diversity of plant structures is best for supporting these generalist predators.	Angelica, baccharis, black-eyed Susan, boltonia, buckwheat, calamint, caraway, chamomile, cilantro, cinquefoil, coreopsis, cosmos, Culver's root, daisies, dill, eriogonum, feverfew, golden alexanders, goldenrod, heliopsis, laceflower, lovage, oregano, phacelia, sweet alyssum, wallflower, and yellow coneflower.

soldier beetles

Various insect eggs and larvae, grasshoppers, caterpillars, aphids, mealybugs, and others

Asters, black-eyed Susans, boltonia, buckwheat, chamomile, cilantro, coreopsis, daisies, goldenrod, oregano, and sunflowers.

spiders

Insect eggs, various beetles, aphids, cutworms, fire ants, plant bugs, spider mites, true bugs, budworms, caterpillars, corn earworms, and many, many other insects

Spiders thrive in a richly diverse environment. Use many different plant structures within the landscape.

tachinid flies

Caterpillars of many kinds, Colorado potato beetles, corn earworms, cucumber beetles, cutworms, earwigs, four-lined plant bugs, true bugs, Japanese beetles, Mexican bean beetles, sawfly larvae, squash bugs, and tobacco budworms

As adults, these parasitoids depend on nectar and pollen. Appropriate plants include angelica, anise, asters, black-eyed Susan, boltonia, boneset, buckwheat, calamint, chamomile, cilantro, cosmos, daisies, dill, eriogonum, feverfew, heliopsis, lovage, oregano, phacelia, sweet alyssum, and yellow coneflower.

the commercial stuff

purchased beneficials, good bug lures, supplemental foods, and seed blends

The beautiful colors and varied textures introduced to your garden through dedicated insectary plantings can create a truly beautiful landscape.

nearly every garden supply catalog that finds its way to my mailbox these days features at least a handful of commercial products dedicated to promoting beneficial insects. Whether it is an artificial food to nourish them, a lure to attract them, or a glass vial filled with the hungry predators themselves, these products are marketed to gardeners as eco-friendly pest control solutions. Though not all of these products prove useful in every garden, they are certainly worth discussing.

This chapter is intended to introduce you to several of these products and enable you to make an informed decision about the potential value of their use within your landscape.

Should you open your wallet to purchase any of them? I'll leave that decision up to you.

purchased beneficials

A few years ago I received an email from someone regarding a praying mantid egg case she had bought at a local nursery. Her family had intended to raise the baby mantids to adulthood, feeding them insects collected from the garden and pet store crickets, and housing them in an old aquarium tank. The author of the letter went on to describe how the mantids had hatched a few weeks later while the family was away for the weekend. The tiny hatchlings had climbed through the screen mesh on top of the aquarium, and the family had come home to hundreds of baby mantids clambering around their house. She said they were finding them for days afterward and putting them back into the aquarium tank, this time with a finer screen on top. But the baby mantids seemed to still be escaping somehow because no matter how many went back into the tank, there were only ever one or two in there by the next morning. Finally they stopped finding baby mantids in the house and tried to rear the remaining two in the aquarium. Her eight-year-old son named the mantids Stretch and Slim and enjoyed feeding and watching them. Then one day he came home from school to find Slim consuming Stretch, head first. It was a valuable lesson, she said, for the entire family. "If you live with someone long enough, you're eventually going to want to bite their head off."

I wrote about the email in my newspaper column, advising her of the importance of separating the baby mantids soon after hatching to prevent cannibalism. I also told readers that if they are ever going to try to raise a mantid in a fish tank, lots of other things must be considered besides what to feed them and the size of the screening on top of the tank. They need a stick positioned diagonally across the tank from which the mantid can hang to molt. They need a water source and a wet sponge in the tank to keep the humidity high. And they need vegetation for the mantid to hide in. I was surprised at the number of comments I got from readers over the next few weeks—everything from "that is so cruel" to "that is so cool."

The most interesting comment came from a man who was considering purchasing a container of mature ladybugs from a garden center. (Some ladybugs sold this way are wild collected, while some are insectary reared; there are pros and cons to each.) He wondered if they too would eventually eat each other so that only one gargantuan ladybug would remain in the container. I got a good chuckle out of his question at first, but when I thought about it, I realized that it wasn't as silly as it had initially seemed (except for the whole idea of a gargantuan ladybug). The rules of the

Adult green lacewings are ready for release from this jar into a garden or greenhouse.

insect world are akin to "eat or be eaten," and I suppose that if the ladybugs were left in the container long enough—*and* if they were not kept in the refrigerator as per the instructions, *and* if the ladybugs consumed all the artificial food in the container, *and* if they managed to not die of dehydration—they just might turn to each other as a food source. But I really didn't think it was likely to happen, and so I told him as much.

Intraguild predation among ladybugs is a common occurrence; however, it more frequently occurs between different species

Hungry lacewing larvae are also sometimes packaged in the folds of corrugated cardboard sealed with translucent fabric sheeting that must be peeled back. Here the lacewing larvae are being used to control whiteflies attacking flowering tobacco plants.

and different life stages (for example, an Asian ladybug adult will readily consume the larvae of a seven-spotted ladybug). That being said, when it comes to a container full of hungry ladybugs, it's anyone's bet. I'm sharing this story because most gardeners, at one time or another, are offered the opportunity to purchase live beneficial insects.

The practice of purchasing and releasing natural enemies into a landscape or a greenhouse to keep pest populations in check is known as augmentative biological control or augmentation. Though this approach is seldom a permanent solution to a pest problem, it does lead to an increase—albeit often a brief one—in the population of that particular predator or parasitoid. When you release those ladybugs, for example, there is no guarantee they are going to stick around. They will go wherever they can find the resources they need to survive. If you want to improve the chances of an introduced natural enemy taking up residence, you need to ensure all the resources it needs are already present. This is true in a garden as well as in the contained environment of a greenhouse, where controlled releases of natural enemies can prove especially beneficial. In both situations, prey and/or hosts need to be available along with any necessary plant-based nutrition.

Augmentation can occur via two different approaches. The first is an inundative release in which large numbers of natural enemies are introduced in order to flood the environment and immediately reduce pest numbers. It is generally performed when pest numbers have already reached an unacceptable level. Releasing that container of ladybugs around an aphid-infested plant is an example of an inundative release. Inoculative releases, on the other hand, involve repeated releases of smaller numbers of natural enemies timed at various intervals, often beginning when pest numbers are very low. The goal of this approach is to keep pest numbers at a tolerable level throughout the season and provide more long-term control. It serves to prevent an unacceptable injury level from occurring in the first place. Inoculative releases of predatory mites and other natural enemies most often take place in greenhouses and conservatories.

Companies that raise the beneficial insects intended for release are known as insectaries. They are fascinating operations capable of rearing hundreds of thousands of natural enemies, at all life stages at any given time. Through these companies, growers have access to dozens of different predators and

Inoculative releases of the parasitoid *Aphytis melinus* take place in some California citrus orchards to combat California red scale.

parasitoids as eggs, larvae, pupae, or adults. Most of these companies are more than happy to work with growers to determine which species is most appropriate for release and at what stage in the insect's life cycle it's best to release it. It's important to remember that the home range of larvae is smaller than that of most winged adults, so they are more likely to stick around. But larvae are also more vulnerable to predators and starvation. That's where relying on the knowledge and experience of the insectary comes into play.

In the years before having both an insectary border and an appreciation for all the beneficial insects already living in my own landscape, I introduced insectary-reared lacewing eggs, lacewing larvae, praying mantid eggs, ladybugs, trichogramma wasps, and predatory mites into my garden. Each was targeted at a particular pest infestation. Can

Tiny parasitoids (*Trichogramma pretiosum*) have parasitized the moth eggs glued to these plastic strips. To introduce these parasitic wasps to the garden or greenhouse, the gardener simply tears off a strip and hangs it in the garden.

Insectary-reared natural enemies come neatly packaged with appropriate instructions and materials for their release. Here is a small sampling of the many beneficials available from one my favorite insectaries, Rincon-Vitova in Ventura, California.

I say that they were an unequivocal success? With the possible exception of the lacewing larvae (who, much to my satisfaction, rapidly wiped out the whiteflies infesting my nicotiana plants), certainly not. Do I think they helped? Maybe. Did they hurt anything? Absolutely not. Choosing to purchase and release natural enemies into an open landscape is an act of faith.

For most home gardeners, natural enemy releases, whether inundative or inoculative, aren't always practical. And that's precisely why creating an insectary habitat to fulfill the nutritional needs of your indigenous natural enemies is so important. You won't have to spend money to purchase good bugs when so many are already taking up residence on their own and naturally keeping pest numbers in

check. But until your insectary border is up and operational and taking care of business as it should, know that augmentation with purchased beneficials is an environmentally sound way to help keep pests in check.

supplemental foods

In addition to live beneficial insects and synthetic lures, gardeners may also be presented with the opportunity to buy supplemental foods for their beneficial insects. Additional food sources like these are known to enhance the survivorship, growth, and development of certain beneficials, including spiders, lacewings, and ladybugs. Judicious applications of supplemental foods are of particular value at times when nectar and pollen are scarce.

luring in the beneficials

Based on an interview with Ian Kaplan, PhD, assistant professor of entomology at Purdue University, West Lafayette, Indiana

IN ADDITION TO SUPPLEMENTING populations of natural enemies through augmentative releases, it's possible to manipulate existing populations of beneficials through the use of semiochemicals. As you'll recall, semiochemicals are volatile signals released into the air by plants that enable them to communicate with insects and with each other. The semiochemicals released by plants when they are being damaged by herbivorous insects are known as herbivore-induced plant volatiles (HIPVs). Part of the role of these compounds is to serve as a sort of signal to predators and parasitoids, luring them to the plant in order to help control pests. Scientists like Ian Kaplan are examining several different ways humans can manipulate beneficial insects via the use of HIPVs.

Employing synthetic HIPVs to recruit natural enemies is one technique that's already in regular use. Another involves using applications of a synthetic plant hormone to induce increased emissions of natural HIPVs from a treated plant, and a third technique involves breeding or genetically engineering plants to enhance levels of HIPVs. "Each of these techniques has different benefits and drawbacks—and there are lots of trade-offs and questions about each of them," begins Kaplan.

The synthetic HIPVs already being employed by growers are used to draw predators and parasitoids to a particular area. The presence of these compounds mimics a plant's response to a large number of pests and induces prey- and host-seeking activities among many predators and parasitoids. This is currently done primarily through the use of controlled-release dispensers of a commercially produced, artificial HIPV attractant. Its active ingredient is methyl salicylate (MeSA), a synthetic HIPV known to attract many different species of natural enemies, including ladybugs, syrphid flies, lacewings, predatory bugs, predatory mites, and others.

"The benefit of using artificial HIPVs is that you can use them at whatever level you want and for however long you want. They are very flexible," explains Kaplan. But there are also some drawbacks. For example, evidence suggests that natural enemies respond to a particular HIPV because they have learned to associate that specific chemical cue with a reward (a juicy pest for lunch). Using synthetic HIPVs in a situation where no reward is in place may backfire and teach beneficials *not* to associate these cues with food. Essentially, we are baiting the good bugs with the promise of food, but if the food isn't there, they may learn to ignore that signal in the future.

In hopes of avoiding this problem, some scientists are examining an attract-and-reward strategy that involves combining the use of artificial HIPVs in a crop field with a nearby flowering border to ensure that at least some plant-based nutrition is present as a reward. The theory is that it will keep the insects around, even if their prey or host insects aren't present. Field test results haven't yet borne this out, but researchers are still working on it.

Another issue with artificial HIPVs, according to Kaplan, is the lack of evidence that products like this do anything more than increase the population of natural enemies. Artificial HIPV attractants are marketed to home gardeners, and evidence shows that it does in fact lure in beneficials. But whether it keeps them there and whether they are actually eating more pests are still open questions.

One more issue regarding the use of artificial HIPVs relates to the complex secrets of nature. "Natural HIPVs are an incredibly complex blend of compounds with an infinite number of combinations, and the plants that produce them can choose when to release them and how much of them to release," Kaplan explains. Beneficials respond not only to a given compound or combination of compounds but also to their ratio within the semiochemical, resulting in an infinite number of possibilities. How will scientists ever know which combination will yield which results? For now, only the plants and insects have those answers.

Herbivore-induced plant volatiles (HIPVs) are released by certain plants as they are being attacked by pest insects. Predators and parasitoids, like this parasitic wasp, are drawn to these signals, which humans are beginning to use to manipulate the behavior of beneficials.

Kaplan envisions a day when plants are labeled for their ability to attract beneficial insects based on the level of HIPVs they naturally produce. Because a lot of natural variation exists among plants regarding HIPV emissions, that will be useful information for gardeners as they try to choose between, say, tomato or pepper varieties. Gardeners will be able to select varieties based not just on taste or yield but also on their ability to lure in natural enemies.

Then there is the concept of using genetically engineered plants to manipulate beneficial insects. According to Kaplan, researchers have found that many North American corn varieties are completely deficient in certain HIPVs,

Artificial HIPVs are already being used to attract beneficial insects to parts of the landscape. The white plastic vial attached to the stake in this photo is the lure, and the yellow sticky card placed above it is used by Kaplan and his team to monitor species of beneficials drawn to the lure.

perhaps as a result of many decades of breeding. These researchers have discovered that they can restore the HIPV signals by reintroducing the gene that produces them. But Kaplan cautions that this raises some important issues. Turning on the HIPV production gene means that the plant is always producing the signal. "If the signal is always on, will the beneficials eventually adapt and learn that there is not necessarily a reward when they respond to the signal? How do we use these semiochemicals without attracting more pests? How do we do it without deterring pollinators? How do we do all this without interfering with everything else? It's a challenge that we are really just beginning to examine."

As you can see, Kaplan's field of research is full of questions. And promise. "Humans can't smell or otherwise detect all these signals. It's so cryptic to us," he says. "And that is exactly what makes it so fascinating."

Commercially available brands of beneficial insect food include BioControl Honeydew from Ladies in Red, Good Bug Power Meal from Arbico Organics, and Good Bug Food from Peaceful Valley Farm Supply, among others.

These and other supplemental foods are intended to attract more beneficials to a particular area, as well as to keep the number of existing beneficials consistent by preventing their departure. They are based on yeasts and sugars and are applied as a spray or as a paste painted onto wooden stakes positioned throughout the garden or field. Some of the more commonly available beneficial insect foods are made of wheast, a combination of yeast and milk whey (a byproduct of cheese making), and must be combined with sugar or honey and diluted with water before application. Amino acids such as tryptophan are present in the wheast and serve to attract more beneficials than plain sugar-water sprays (more on these soon).

If you don't want to purchase one of these commercially made foods, you can make a homemade version (minus the whey). Mix ½ cup sugar, 2 teaspoons honey, 4 tablespoons brewer's yeast, and ⅔ cup water. Then dilute 2 tablespoons of this concoction with 1 quart warm water and spray it on plants whenever you have a pest issue and want to lure in more beneficials. The undiluted mixture stores in the fridge for a week or two.

In addition to yeast-based foods, a simple sugar-water solution consisting of 5 ounces sugar to 1 quart water can be sprayed on crops to cause rapid aggregation of ladybugs and certain other beneficials—although it is shown to be less attractive to beneficials than wheast-based sprays. Beneficials tend to hang out longer in fields sprayed with sugar water than they do in untreated control plots. Ladybug densities are at least 50 to 77 percent higher in sugar-sprayed areas, and such an application may also increase the numbers of other types of beneficials. Sugar-water sprays are, in essence, an artificial version of honeydew, a valuable carbohydrate source for many beneficials. Do be aware, though, that using sugar-water sprays and/or wheast-based foods may also increase the number of ants, earwigs, and other opportunistic feeders that come to the garden.

Sugar sprays can also be used to manipulate the movements of natural enemies by encouraging them to move into pest-infested areas more quickly. But even the increased presence of beneficials when supplemental foods are in place never guarantees higher rates of predation and parasitism.

seed blends

A number of readily available commercial seed blends are targeted at providing appropriate pollen and nectar sources for beneficials.

These seed mixes consist of a collection of plants intended to support a diversity of beneficials throughout the year. Some of the mixes comprise annuals only, while others include perennials, ground covers, and even grasses. They are a good choice for gardeners wanting to support more natural enemies without building a formal insectary garden.

The number of natural enemies present in and around areas where these seed mixes are planted depends on factors from weed competition and the weather to prey populations, the maturity of the plants themselves, and the presence of good overwintering sites. Monitored tomato plants interplanted with one of these seed blends showed no increase in the predation rates of hornworms and tomato fruit worms versus a control plot interplanted only with millet. But a season-long increase in plant-dwelling spiders and big-eyed bugs was found in areas planted with insectary seed blends adjacent to plots of turfgrass. Quantifying the predation rates for pest insects as a result of installing these seed blends is very difficult. What we do know, though, is that when a diversity of flowering plants is on hand, we often see an increase in the numbers and diversity of beneficial insects.

At North Carolina State University in 2003, several different seed blends were compared for seed purity as well as for their beneficial insect–luring prowess. Good Bug Blend from Peaceful Valley Farm Supply was found to host the highest population of parasitoids and predators. In addition to this seed collection, a handful of others are on the market, including several regionally specific blends, with some even tailored for growth height and intended use. Rincon-Vitova Insectary in Ventura, California, offers a number of seed blends, including Beneficial Blend Seed Mix, Insecta-Flora (also available in a low-growing mix), and Interflora (a blend specifically created to be part of vegetable intercropping). Arbico Organics carries Good Bug Flowering Beneficial Insect Habitat, Johnny's Selected Seeds has Beneficial Insect Attractant Mix, and Gurney's provides a mix named Beneficial Bug Blend. And this is just a small sampling of the seed blends intended to promote and support numerous beneficials. Using one of these seed mixes, or any of the commercial products I just highlighted, may lead to a better, longer life for your beneficials.

Insects, along with everything else in nature, introduce uncertainty and unpredictability into our lives. Perhaps that's why we humans often find ourselves afraid of or repulsed by them. Most of us prefer order and fact to uncertainty and unpredictability. It's what we do when we garden, isn't it? We try to bring our own sense of order and organization to nature. What we fail to realize is that nature was already in perfect order. Before our meddling hands became part of the equation, each natural ecosystem operated flawlessly. But now it is impossible to take ourselves out of the equation. We've been messing with nature for thousands of years and there is no way we can put it back the way it was.

What we *can* do is recognize and nurture the natural order of our own tiny bit of the world. Bring the insect life back into your yard and garden and with it will come a multitude of positives, the most important of which is balance. I'm not asking you to find slug love

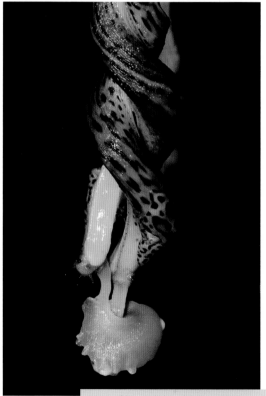

A pair of leopard slugs hangs in their nocturnal embrace.

as fascinating as I do, nor am I asking you to change everything about how you garden. I'm asking you to allow the amazing creatures that live and breathe and work in your garden to stay. Allow them to do what they evolved to do. Allow yourself to appreciate and admire and foster them, even if society tells you that you're supposed to find them vile and malevolent. You know now that most of them are just the opposite. They are charismatic, fascinating, and so very beneficial; and, sadly, many of them are running out of time. Extinction is on the horizon for thousands of insect species around the world. Do what you can to provide sanctuary to these small creatures. Get to know them, watch them, discover how truly valuable they are. Let them do their amazing work.

So I end the book at the same place I started it—with slug sex and David Attenborough.

"These two worlds—ours and theirs—influence one another to an extraordinary degree. If we and the rest of the backboned animals were to disappear overnight, the rest of the world would get on pretty well. But if they were to disappear, the land's ecosystems would collapse. For the fact is, they were the pioneers; the first animals of any kind to colonize the lands of the Earth."
—David Attenborough, *Life in the Undergrowth*

resources

• • • • • • • • • • • • • • • • • • • •

Suppliers of beneficial insects and related products

Arbico Organics
P. O. Box 8910
Tucson, AZ 85738
800-827-2847
www.arbico-organics.com

American Insectaries, Inc.
30805 Rodriguez Road
Escondido, CA 92026
760-751-1436
www.americaninsectaries.com

Beneficial Insectary, Inc.
9664 Tanqueray Ct.
Redding, CA 96003
800-477-3715
www.insectary.com

Beneficial Insect Company
244 Forrest Street
Fort Mill, SC 29715
803-547-2301
www.thebeneficialinsectco.com

Biofac, Inc.
P. O. Box 87
Mathis, TX 78368
800-233-4914
www.biofac.com

BioLogic Company
Springton Road, P. O. Box 177
Willow Hill, PA 17271
717-349-2789
www.biologicco.com

Buglogical Control Systems
P. O. Box 32046
Tucson, AZ 85751
520-298-4400
www.buglogical.com

Gardener's Supply Company
128 Intervale Road
Burlington, VT 05401
800-876-5520
www.gardeners.com

Gardens Alive!
5100 Schenley Place
Lawrenceburg, IN 47025
513-354-1483
www.gardensalive.com

Gurney's
P. O. Box 4178
Greendale, IN 47025
513-354-1492
www.gurneys.com

Johnny's Selected Seeds
P. O. Box 299
Waterville, ME 04903
877-564-6697
www.johnnyseeds.com

Peaceful Valley Farm Supply
P. O. Box 2209
Grass Valley, CA 95945
888-784-1722
www.groworganic.com

Planet Natural
1612 Gold Avenue
Bozeman, MT 59715
800-289-6656
www.planetnatural.com

Rincon-Vitova Insectaries, Inc.
108 Orchard Drive
Ventura, CA 93001
800-248-2847
www.rinconvitova.com

• •
Soil test purveyors

Soil tests are available from your local agricultural extension service—a service run by land-grant university agriculture departments to provide the public with information about farming and gardening. To find the extension service nearest you, visit www.extension.org *or* www.csrees.usda.gov/extension. You may also find it listed in the blue (government) pages of your local phone book, usually in the county government section.

Soil tests are also available from the following independent labs:

Brookside Laboratories, Inc.
308 South Main St.
New Knoxville, OH 45871
419-753-2448
www.blinc.com

Peaceful Valley Farm Supply
P. O. Box 2209
Grass Valley, CA 95945
888-784-1722
www.groworganic.com

Soiltest Farm Consultants, Inc.
2925 Driggs Drive
Moses Lake, WA 98837
509-765-1622
www.soiltestlab.com

Waters Agricultural Laboratories
2101 Highway 81
Owensboro, KY 42301
270-685-4039
www.watersag.com

further reading

Buchmann, Stephen L., and Gary Paul Nabhan. 1997. *The Forgotten Pollinators.* Washington, DC: Island Press.

Cranshaw, Whitney. 2004. *Garden Insects of North America: The Ultimate Guide to Backyard Bugs.* Princeton, NJ: Princeton University Press.

Eaton, Eric R., and Kenn Kaufman. 2007. *Kaufman Field Guide to Insects of North America.* Boston: Houghton Mifflin Harcourt.

Flint, Mary Louise, and Steve H. Driestadt. 1999. *Natural Enemies Handbook: The Illustrated Guide to Biological Pest Control.* Berkeley, CA: University of California Press.

Grissell, Eric. 2010. *Bees, Wasps, and Ants: The Indispensable Role of Hymenoptera in Gardens.* Portland, OR: Timber Press.

———. 2001. *Insects and Gardens: In Pursuit of a Garden Ecology.* Portland, OR: Timber Press.

Hajek, Ann E. 2004. *Natural Enemies: An Introduction to Biological Control.* Cambridge, UK: Cambridge University Press.

Olkowski, William, Sheila Daar, and Helga Olkowski with Steven Ash. 2013. *The Gardener's Guide to Common-Sense Pest Control*, revised ed. Newtown, CT: Taunton Press.

Tallamy, Douglas. 2009. *Bringing Nature Home: How You Can Sustain Wildlife with Native Plants*, updated and expanded ed. Portland, OR: Timber Press.

acknowledgments

I owe a debt of gratitude, first and foremost, to the men and women who dedicate their professional lives to understanding the never-ending intricacies of the insect world. I am especially grateful to those who have graciously allowed me to interview them for inclusion in this text but also wish to extend a hearty "thank you" to those who contributed photographs and answered my many questions. It is with great admiration and appreciation that I thank the following scientists for their contribution to the creation of this book as well as for their inspiration: Leslie Allee, Robert Bugg, Scott Creary, Rex Dufour, Gwendolyn Ellen, Dan Herms, Ian Kaplan, Joseph Patt, Mike Raupp, Paula Shrewsbury, and Doug Tallamy.

During the writing process, I was fortunate enough to be able to rely on two kindred spirits for their advice and proofreading prowess. To Jeanne Poremski and Scott Creary, I tip my hat. Your advice on the book's organization, clarity, and factuality is so very appreciated!

For their help in locating plants to photograph, I thank John Totten, Kathy McGregor, Brian Shema, Randy Soergel, Noah Petronic, Martha Swiss, Jim Bonner, Denise Schreiber, and Dianne Machesney.

Heather Orient of Orient Outdoor Designs, I cannot thank you enough for being such a quick draw. Your help with the garden designs and layouts was invaluable . . . and fun.

Thank you to Juree Sondker and the rest of the gang at Timber Press for believing in this book—and in me. It has been a true pleasure working with you, and I am grateful for your knowledge, gently conveyed suggestions, and faith.

To Lorraine Anderson, my careful and thoughtful editor: your professionalism has truly astounded me and your gentle guidance and kind words are so very much appreciated. I am grateful to have had the opportunity to work with you. Let's do it again someday!

I would be remiss if I neglected to thank Paul Wiegman, for he was the man who started it all; and Doug Oster, the man who keeps it rolling. I owe you both dinner. But not together. Because that would be trouble.

And last, to my patient and supportive husband, John: sorry about all the containers of insects in the fridge, all the research papers scattered across the dining room table, all the distracting photography road trips, all my ineptitude with computer-related issues, and all the times I ran inside to grab my camera because some robber fly finally landed. You are one forgiving man (I hope, anyway).

index

photography credits

Agenturfotograf/iStockphoto, page 153 bottom right
Anderson, Robert L., USDA Forest Service, bugwood.org, pages 47 top, 207 left
Berger, Joseph, bugwood.org, pages 43 left, 202 right
Bryson, Charles T., USDA Agricultural Research Service, bugwood.org, page 150 left
Cardillo, Rob, Beaubaire garden, pages 169, 170, 171, 176
Cardina, John, Ohio State Weed Lab Archive, The Ohio State University, page 160 bottom
Cranshaw, Whitney, Colorado State University, bugwood.org, page 105
Ellen, Gwendolyn, pages 174, 199 left, 199 right, 201
Evans, Chris, Illinois Wildlife Action Plan, bugwood.org, pages 160 top, 194 left
Hermes, Catherine, Ohio State Weed Lab Archive, page 144 top
Holt, Saxon, pages 2, 7, 10–11, 38–39, 86–87, 108–109, 117 left, 146 right, 147 bottom,
    164–165, 168, 175, 188–189, 191, 192, 193, 196, 210–211
Kaplan, Ian, page 218
Lotz, Jeffrey W., Florida Department of Agriculture, bugwood.org, page 23
Moorehead, Cheryl, bugwood.org, page 75
Old, Richard, XID Services, Inc., bugwood.org, page 155 bottom left
Ottens, Russ, University of Georgia, bugwood.org, pages 43 right, 48–49
Person, Birte, page 221
Rawlins, Karan A., University of Georgia, bugwood.org, pages 121 right, 144 bottom
Schwartz, Howard F., Colorado State University, bugwood.org, page 190
Shepard, Merle, Gerald Carner, and P.A.C. Ooi, bugwood.org, page 57 bottom
Spivey, Terry, USDA Forest Service, bugwood.org, page 116
Turner, Mark, page 197
Verhasselt, Elmer, bugwood.org, page 72
Webster, Theodore, Ohio State Weed Lab Archive, page 155 bottom right
Wray, Paul, Iowa State University, bugwood.org, page 103

All other photos are by the author.

KRISTY KROUSE

about the author

Jessica Walliser cohosts *The Organic Garden-ers* on KDKA radio in Pittsburgh, Pennsylvania. Her column "The Good Earth" appears twice weekly in the Pittsburgh *Tribune-Review*, and she is a regular contributor to *Fine Gardening*, *Urban Farm*, *Popular Farming*, *Hobby Farms*, and *Hobby Farm Home* magazines. She was formerly a contributing editor at *Organic Gardening* magazine. Jessica is also heard on Essential Public Radio's environmental news program, and she lectures at garden clubs, botanic gardens, arboretums, and other public garden facilities across the United States.

Jessica received her degree in ornamental horticulture from Pennsylvania State University and is the former owner of a 25-acre organic market farm. She also serves on the faculty of Phipps Conservatory and Botanical Gardens. The author of three other organic gardening books, Jessica lives and gardens on 2 acres northwest of Pittsburgh, Pennsylvania, with her husband, John; son, Ty; one dog, six chickens, three goldfish, and billions and billions of very good bugs.

Connect with Jessica by visiting her website and Bug Blog at jessicawalliser.com.